Meat Pots
Manna
and a
Merciful God

Meat Pots
Manna
and a
Merciful God

Exchanging the Wilderness *for* PROMISE

KATIE MEADOWS

Victoria, Australia

Copyright © 2022 by Katie Meadows

All rights reserved. No part of this publication may be reproduced, distributed or transmitted in any form or by any means, including photocopying, recording, or other electronic or mechanical methods, without the prior written permission of the publisher, except in the case of brief quotations embodied in critical reviews and certain other non-commercial uses permitted by copyright law.

For permission and order requests, please contact the publisher.
Journey Publishing
PO Box 6066
White Hills, VIC, Australia 3550
journeypublishing@outlook.com

The author has made a deliberate literary decision to use lowercase when referring to the spoken and written word of God. This differentiates such occasions from references to the person of Jesus, known as the Word, and is consistent with commonly used Bible translations.

Unless otherwise noted, all Scripture taken from the New King James Version®. Copyright © 1982 by Thomas Nelson. Used by permission. All rights reserved.

Acknowledgement to the following publishers and translations, as they appear in the text:

Scripture quotations taken from the Amplified® Bible (AMP), Copyright © 2015 by The Lockman Foundation. Used by permission. www.lockman.org. Scripture quotations taken from the (NASB®) New American Standard Bible®, Copyright © 1960,1971,1977,1995 by The Lockman Foundation. Used by permission. All rights reserved. www.lockman.org. Scripture quotations marked NLT are taken from the *Holy Bible*, New Living Translation, copyright © 1996, 2004, 2015 by Tyndale House Foundation. Used by permission of Tyndale House Publishers, Inc., Carol Stream, Illinois 60188. All rights reserved. Scripture quotations marked TPT are from The Passion Translation®. Copyright © 2017, 2018, 2020 by Passion & Fire Ministries, Inc. Used by permission. All rights reserved. ThePassionTranslation.com.

Meat pots, Manna, and a Merciful God / Katie Meadows. 1st ed.
A catalogue record for this book is available from the National Library of Australia.
ISBN: 978-0-6489634-0-0
ISBN: 978-0-6489634-1-7 (e-book)

Dedication

I dedicate this book to my much-loved family and to those who inspire me to keep going and grasp for higher truths.

Many have influenced, encouraged, and taught me in the ways of God throughout my life. I appreciate all of you.

My Teacher deserves my highest praise.

A Psalm of Rescue

He reached down from heaven and rescued me;
he drew me out of deep waters.
He rescued me from my powerful enemies,
from those who hated me and were too strong for me.

They attacked me at a moment when I was in distress,
*but the L*ORD *supported me.*
He led me to a place of safety;
he rescued me because he delights in me.

Psalm 18:16–19 NLT

Contents

Preface ix
Introduction 1
1. Promise-keeper 5
2. The Charm of Egypt 13
3. How Did We Get Here? 19
4. Enemy Tactics 25
5. God's Children in Bondage? 35
6. Salvation Is at Hand 47
7. The Lessons of Passover 55
8. Red Sea Baptism 65
9. Questioning God's Provision 77
10. Testing and Mocking God 87
11. Bones in the Wilderness 99
12. Fire and Sacrifice 107
13. Stuck on the Threshold 117
14. Jesus, the Fulfilment 125
15. A New Generation 137
16. Crossing Over (finally)! 143
17. Mt Gerizim and Mt Ebal 151
18. The Curse-breaker 163
19. A God of Blessings 171
20. We Are the Mouthpiece of God 181
21. Taking Ground 191

22. Fighting Giants 201
23. Walking in Inheritance 211
24. Our Final Promise 221
    Notes 227

Preface

The invitation to write this book didn't come from a friend, a pastor, or an article I read. It came unexpectedly and after years of preparation. First, there was a nudge to seek God for myself, and not in a second-hand manner through my local church. When I dug into the word of God, I unearthed treasures. I discovered that when I read the Scriptures, God would speak to me. Imagine that. The God of all creation wanting to speak to little old me! I discovered that He delights in sharing His wisdom, and He patiently waits until we desire to learn from Him. He waited a long time to get my attention. I was a good church-girl. But I was not truly God's girl. He was out of my league, and rather scary (that was shame and religion talking).

The Holy Spirit's nudge was the catalyst to wake me up in my pew. How many of us have fallen asleep? Some of us are so churched that we could deliver the sermon word for word and quote the books of the Bible backwards. But as I learned, God doesn't want parrots. He wants brave and radical followers of Jesus who are willing to look foolish to a dying world. Would I be fool enough? Would I risk losing whatever comfortable religious existence I had to tune into the still, small voice of the Spirit?

It's been a decade since I felt the discomfit of pew dwelling. I am not saying sitting on pews is a bad thing. But God knew the pull of religion in my life was strong, so in His mercy, He moved me to revive me. I remember thinking, 'There has to be more than this'. I craved more than church attendance and compliance with perceived expectations. That unsettling question was the beginning of a transformative life-process. Back then, I didn't know I was a spiritual captive, needing to be set free.

After applying myself to God's word for around seven years, the concept for this book started swirling around inside me. I read the stories of the Israelites with fresh eyes. Their captivity, God's miraculous rescue, and a string of failures and victories jumped off the pages. I read and journaled. After two years of immersing myself in these stories, this book fell onto the pages. There was an urgency to write. As I wrote, I noted the similarities of my spiritual experience with those of my characters. I had trekked my wilderness for the best part of forty years. Oh, how sad that is! All that time, my answer was in front of me, beckoning me with His love and outstretched hand to accept His invitation.

Some of us learn more slowly than others. To be fair, being stuck in a religious mindset is like wearing an iron band around your head, but you don't know you're wearing it. You don't realise that it's sucking the life out of you and is the reason for the dull ache you cannot be free of. One day, someone unlocks the band with a special key and you experience life without it for the first time. Your senses come alive and your fears melt away. Truth and understanding, previously hidden from you behind a thick veil, are now within your grasp.

Most importantly, the Person of God comes alive to you. He is no longer hidden behind that thick veil. He has torn the veil in two and met you right where you're standing. In fact, the first verse that I remember God highlighting when He invited me to do life with Him was, 'Draw near to God and He will draw near to you' (James 4:8). So, I took a step! It turns out the verse is one hundred percent true.

Now I invite you, dear reader, to take a journey with me. God wrote these words and stories on my heart and invited me to share them. Yes, it is written in my style and with my hand. However, words with life-transformative power can never come from a mere human. If you hear the voice of the Spirit while you read the words on these pages, I strongly encourage you to stop and listen. Never refuse an invitation from God, no matter how small or inconvenient it first appears. I have included plenty of Scriptures and references. You may choose to dig a little deeper for yourself.

I have a deep desire to see you and I step into our God-ordained purpose, where our lives will shine far brighter than if we authored our story alone. Take a journey with me. I pray God will meet you on the well-travelled path.

Introduction

Have you ever heard Christians referring to their 'wilderness experience'? The concept sounded spiritual to me—even noble, until I studied the wild wilderness wanderings of the Israelites. It dawned on me how patient God was with this large group of stiff-necked persons who continually tried His perfect patience. Gulp. Suddenly, my noble spiritual image of a pilgrimage through the wild in restlessness of soul appeared far less desirable. I read about quail and manna, grumbling, and rebellion. The Provider who gave quail until it came out of the people's nostrils also sent plagues as punishment. Now may I ask—who would like a wilderness journey?

I think we often misunderstand wilderness wanderings. We can expect rugged periods during our spiritual journey. Some of these seasons may be described as the 'dark night of the soul'. Sometimes we wander through a barren land not because God led us there, but because we drifted off the path and away from His steady hand. And yes, there will be times of testing and training where we may feel disoriented and without a compass. I'm not suggesting we will never walk a wilderness trail. I'm pulling at the thread that hems our understanding of what a wilderness journey is—and isn't. How should new covenant believers understand the Israelites' personal and spiritual experiences as they journeyed into Promise? This topic holds deep spiritual truths that will enlighten us if we dig them out.

But, have you ever stopped to consider that the God of Israel's fathers never told them He would take them from Egypt through a wilderness? I can find no occasion where God said, 'I will take you from captivity through the wilderness. You need to experience the wilderness, my children, before you get to the land of Promise'. Trust me, I've looked—and I've looked again! This hunt for God's treasures led me to find answers to my questions on this important topic. In fact, I discovered the whole Bible is focused on promise! If you take a helicopter view, you can't miss it. It extends from Genesis chapter 1 to the last chapter of the great Book of Revelation. He is the God of promise.

When the Lord heard the cry of His people under the Egyptian masters' cruel hands, He did not intend to bring them out from captivity to wander through a wilderness for four decades. God's plan was always to fulfil His promise to Abram:

> *I am the* LORD, *who brought you out of Ur of the Chaldeans,* **to give you this land to inherit it.** *(Genesis 15:7, emphasis mine)*

> *Also I give to you and your descendants after you the land in which you are a stranger,* **all the land of Canaan,** *as an everlasting possession; and I will be their God.* (Genesis 17:8, emphasis mine)

To Moses at the burning bush, God outlines His plan to bring His people to a land flowing with milk and honey:

> *I have said I will bring you up out of the affliction of Egypt to the land of the Canaanites and the Hittites and the Amorites and the Perizzites and the Hivites and the Jebusites, to a land* **flowing with milk and honey.** *(Exodus 3:17, emphasis mine)*

The wilderness was never the destination. God always intended to take the Israelites from cruel tyranny to the land of Promise, and the wilderness was the path He chose to get them there (Exodus 13:17–18). God chose this pathway as the better of two options. His people might have melted and run back to Egypt if they had come face to face with the Philistines so early in their journey (Exodus 13:17)! But the people's wilful and rebellious behaviour caused them to go wilderness camping for another thirty-eight years. God promised a land of milk and honey to Abraham's descendants; He did not promise a wilderness. Sadly, the wilderness became a burial field for a generation.

As believers, we may hold up wilderness experiences as some kind of Christian honour or spiritual passage we must walk through on our way to eternity. Is a wilderness experience necessary for a believer's journey? Does everyone have to pass through a wilderness for refining and chastening? Should we use this term as new covenant people? I believe we answer these questions when we intentionally study the exodus story and the pre-promise years.

We must expand the modern mindset we've developed since the cross and Christendom to do so. To be fair, for many of us, this includes the challenge of trying to strain past our Gentile mindset to see the Hebrew story. This story became the story of the Jewish people and the background to the story of our salvation. It's a powerful narrative because the author is none other than the Spirit of God. Are we ready to dive in and hear what He has to say to us today?

If the wilderness represents a place of barrenness and disobedience, are we still keen to have our Christian wilderness experience? The Israelites' story is specific to a time, but it has spiritual significance today. We should honour the story of the Israelites and not diminish it. I am grateful I can learn from this incredible story, with its highs and lows. I prefer to keep away from the lows (including nostrils full of quail).

God promised a land of milk and honey to Abraham's descendants; He did not promise a wilderness.

1

Promise-keeper

Therefore, say to the children of Israel: "I am the LORD; I will bring you out from under the burdens of the Egyptians, I will rescue you from their bondage, and I will redeem you with an outstretched arm and with great judgments. I will take you as My people, and I will be your God. Then you shall know that I am the LORD your God who brings you out from under the burdens of the Egyptians. **And I will bring you into the land which I swore** *to give to Abraham, Isaac, and Jacob; and I will give it to you as a heritage: I am the LORD." (Exodus 6:6–8, emphasis mine)*

As a child, I was sure God had a big stick, and He was out to get me. This God of wrath picture caused me much fear and hopelessness in my faith. How can you trust a God who is monitoring your behaviour, ready to expose you in your sin at any moment? Well, you can't. Somehow, I mixed up Moses and his rod with God. I saw law everywhere, which is the place I lived for many years. If I could just be good, I wouldn't have to worry about the fear and humiliation of punishment. My heart hurts for that girl. She missed out on so much joy. Ironically, the pages that caused me so much fear are now pages I love to study!

Recently, the reality of Abraham being the father of my faith hit me. Although I had some head knowledge of this, I lived as though Moses was the father of my faith. But I don't look to Moses for my faith because Moses is the mediator of a covenant of rules. I tried to live under that covenant for most of my life—a covenant that no longer exists. I recall a childhood song about Father Abraham, who had many sons and daughters, and I am one of them. Although I sang this song and still recall the words today, there was a disconnect between this teaching and my understanding. I had adopted a hybrid faith that held no comfort or power for me to overcome the fears and struggles in my life.

If your faith and belief have been damaged along life's journey as mine were, you need to understand our salvation comes through faith in the Son of God, not through commandments of stone. Thanks to God's mercy and patience, I set myself to studying the story of Israel and could do so once the chains of fear were gone. I believe we need to understand this amazing journey to understand our faith and, most importantly, the God who authored it. The enemy of our souls wants us to see this story through a lens of confusion, fear, or doubt in God's goodness. But like the rest of the Bible, we must choose to put our faith lens on and learn for ourselves with the Holy Spirit as our Teacher.

As we unpack the specific Promise of God to Abraham and His descendants, we find encouraging spiritual truths that apply to us today. I will refer to the Promise with a capital P because it was a big deal! This Promise was multifaceted and personal, but it led to the promise of salvation for all humanity. There will never be another like it. And through this special story, we identify the God of Abraham, Isaac, and Jacob as a promise-keeper. This has not changed.

Let's start at the beginning, with the call to Abram…

A Promise Worth Waiting For

The story of Abram (before God changed his name to Abraham in Genesis 17) is one of faith. God adopted this one-of-a-kind man from Ur and made a profound Promise to him. The Promise contained his inheritance and seemed as distant and unobtainable as the stars. How does a man become a nation, much less multiple nations, when he and his wife cannot produce one heir?

God included Abram's wife Sarai (later named Sarah) in this Promise and told Abram that Sarai would give birth to a son. This was a challenge to Abram and his wife, as Sarai's inability to conceive was only surpassed by her age. Child-bearing was well in her past. When God told the elderly Sarai and her husband they would have their own biological child, poor old Sarai laughed at the idea! It seemed a fantastic notion.

So the couple decided to help God's Promise along (we'd never do that, right?). Sarai encouraged her husband to navigate around the conception issue and continue Abram's lineage through her Egyptian maid, Hagar. However, this was not an acceptable solution to the God who made the Promise (Genesis 17).

God's Promise to Abram was exact, given to a specific man and his wife in a pre-determined time, with particular outcomes and conditions. Its outcome would never be attributed to a happy accident or human intervention.

Not only would this couple have a child in their old age, but God promised Abram countless descendants, described as more than the stars and the sand. And the Promise didn't end there. The Promise focused on land, a place for Abram's descendants to inhabit on Earth and call home. Now, this makes sense to me. If you have been promised that many descendants, you really need somewhere to put them! God is a practical provider.

The detail of this Promise tells us something about the God of Abram. As you read the following specifics of the Promise, understand our God is the same God who birthed a nation through an old man and his wife. Let's observe how the promises of our Father are always good towards His children. You can count on them!

Aspects of the Promise:

1. Abram would become 'exceedingly fruitful' (Genesis 17:6). He wouldn't just be fruitful—he would surpass the normal by a long way.

2. Nations and kings would come from Abram's descendants. God destined them for greatness. Later, when Abram was renamed Abraham, the meaning of his name changed from 'Exalted father' to 'Chief of multitude'.[1] Sarai's name change parallels Abram's. She goes from the barren wife of Genesis 11 to 'Mother of nations' (Genesis 17:16).

3. God will be their God through the establishment of covenant. It would be an everlasting covenant with an everlasting possession (Genesis 17:7–8). It still exists today!

4. When Abram was promised the land of Canaan, he was a stranger in the land (Genesis 17:8). Sound familiar?

5. God later added the detail of milk and honey through Moses (Exodus 3:8). The Promised Land was fertile and good. God still gives good gifts, and we find the abundance of His produce in His creation.

6. He did not give His people second best.

7. The Lord was so keen to ensure Abraham's son and grandson did not forget the family Promise, that He personally re-iterated it to Isaac (Genesis 26) and to Jacob (Genesis 35). I'm sure Abraham would have passed this information on to his son and grandson, but the Lord is a personal God, and this Promise was *very* important.

And I will establish My covenant between Me and you and your descendants after you in their generations, for an everlasting covenant, to be God to you and your descendants after you. (Genesis 17:7)

Signs of Hope

Tucked away in Scripture is a hint of the future Promise. Abraham purchased a plot of land from a man named Ephron. The plot contained a field with a cave for him to bury his wife, Sarah. Abraham insisted he pay for this land, despite the protestation of the local men that 'prince' Abraham could use one of their choicest burial plots (Genesis 23). My point here is Abraham now legitimately owns a plot of land in Canaan. He will be buried there, along with his son and grandson after him.

Growing up in a small town in Australia, my family wasn't considered genuinely local. My parents moved to our hometown just before my birth. To be a genuine local (which was even joked about) required a couple of previous generations in the local cemetery! Notice when the children of Israel arrived in the land of Promise, there were several generations of ancestors laid to rest there, staking a claim. The bones of Joseph would shortly join them. I find this little detail far more than accidental.

While we can always trust God to be our Promise-keeper, He included conditions in the covenant between Him and His people. The outward expression of Abram's covenant was in the circumcision of all the males of his family, including his future descendants. The 'cutting off of the flesh' involved in circumcision reveals a spiritual reality, but it also symbolises the sanctification of human seed—which speaks of future generations. God set up a holiness principle for His chosen people even before He gave the commandments to Moses. Circumcision also represents a setting apart, which is what holiness does. It sets the children of God apart from the children of the world.

While the covenant God made with His chosen people involved a non-negotiable physical act, we are told circumcision of the heart is the most important requirement before God for both Jew and Gentile (Romans 2:28–29). Doesn't that sound painful? I have some experience with heart circumcision, and I am grateful for God's mercy towards me as He patiently waited and walked me through this long process (still going!). The good news for us is God has already provided for this spiritual circumcision. He gives us all the strength and encouragement we need to pursue His righteousness and cut out the things in our lives that build barriers to our relationship with God—the sins and barriers of the heart. An essential point to understand is these heart barriers also keep us from our promise.

More to Come

What an exciting thing to realise the God of Abraham, Isaac, and Jacob is the God of Jesus Christ, and He's the same yesterday, today, and forever. This means He is neither random nor disposed to change his mind or disappoint us by not coming through, unlike humans prone to breaking our promises. Sometimes we miss out on our promise, not because God is holding out on us, but because we are not positioning ourselves to receive from Him. He will fulfil His promises one way or another. But *we* may miss out because we haven't partnered with Him to produce the outcome. This is what happened to the first generation that came out of Egypt.

As we travel through the wilderness pages in this book, remember—there is a happy ending to the story! The wilderness is not our inheritance. If we are living there, it is time to review our spiritual position. It is not your destiny to inhabit the dry and barren lands.

Jesus stated it best:

But I have come to give you everything in abundance, more than you expect—life in its fullness until you **overflow***!* (John 10:10 TPT, emphasis mine)

I came that they may have and enjoy life, ***and have it in abundance*** *[to the full, till it overflows].* (John 10:10 AMP)

What did God say about the land of Promise? He said it would *flow* with milk and honey. Scripture reveals the principle of obedience and blessing repeatedly. I'm not talking about a cheap prosperity doctrine here! I'm talking about the reality of what Scripture states in outrageous statements such as 'my cup overflows' (Psalm 23) and 'your vats will overflow with new wine' (Proverbs 3:10). This fullness is holistic, encompassing our physical, spiritual, emotional, and mental functions.

It is not your destiny to inhabit the dry and barren lands.

Blessing may be one of the least understood aspects of the Christian faith. Yes, that's a bold statement, but I believe blessing is a necessary concept to understand because our God is the God of blessing. God's promise to Abram was an extensive blessing for all the generations after him and one that culminated (but hasn't ended) in the Person of Jesus Christ. The blessing of Jesus Christ is a never-ending, ever-flowing fountain of Living Water available to refresh our thirsty souls and spirits.

We will come back to the topic of promise later. For now, grasp firmly on the truth that our God is a promise-keeper. And this applies to YOU right now!

> *God is not a man, so he does not lie. He is not human, so he does not change his mind. Has he ever spoken and failed to act? Has he ever promised and not carried it through?* (Numbers 23:19 NLT)

2

The Charm of Egypt

It may be easy to shake our head at Israel's delayed journey across the wilderness, brought about by their grumbling and disobedience. Perhaps we have felt puzzled, even annoyed, at some of the Israelites' behaviours along the way! But a superficial reading of their story could cause us to be harsh in our judgement towards them. What caused a group of rescued slaves to yearn for their past in the place that despised and used them? I doubt we can fully comprehend the Israelites' story without first understanding where they came from.

Between God's Promise to Abraham and the Promised Land stands the ancient civilisation of Egypt. She was a global powerhouse. Like most ancient cultures, she was founded on the worship of gods associated with the created elements. Egyptians centred their worship around a sun god and added many other gods associated with each area of life. For around four centuries, Abraham's descendants were immersed in her culture. And during this period, they experienced an acute level of captivity. The physical, spiritual, and mental impact of long-term slavery and immersion in a dominant, pagan culture may explain their constant mistrust of their Rescuer.

An Ancient Mega-power

My husband has been interested in Egyptology over the years, so I didn't have to look far for information about Egypt of the Israelites' day. A few steps from my desk to our bookcase, and I was in business. For those of you who love history or are interested in ancient Egypt, you can chase up the references I've provided—but if you couldn't wait to exit history class in school, chapter three is coming! As you read this chapter, try to picture the big, bold, and dominant place that was ancient Egypt. Imagine her streets, markets, and temples. And put yourself in the vulnerable shoes of Jacob's descendants.

Egypt's culture and power influenced not only the life and faith practices of the children of Promise, but it also has a ripple effect on us today.

We know ancient Egypt for her longevity. Her power survived multiple dynasties from as early as the fourth millennium BC[1] to the Greek-Egyptian period of Cleopatra's era, ending around 30 BC.[2] How many world powers can claim that kind of history? Many great cultures have come and gone, but few have left such an impact. In fact, Egypt's culture and power influenced not only the life and faith practices of the children of Promise, but it also has a ripple effect on us today.

Egypt's governance and belief system operated on a framework of gods served by the pharaoh—a high priest assigned semi-divine status.[3] Even the royal family sat far beneath the pharaoh in the social structure.[4] Like the power wielded by kings and queens of the Middle

Ages, the ancient pharaohs ruled with absolute power. The stories of Joseph and Moses reveal the authority of these kings.

A pharaoh's most important duty was to maintain the concept of rightness or *maat*, which is a strong Egyptian belief in truth, order, justice, and maintaining the status quo.[5] The opposite of maat is chaos, which the Egyptians devoutly avoided.[6] I believe maat is a key to Egypt's longevity. As long as she kept the power status quo, she retained her position.

Archaeological finds, such as King Tut's tomb, reveal showy displays of wealth for Egyptian nobility. Imagine having an entire pyramid as your burial place! The concept of an afterlife is evident in the way Egyptians built and furnished their pyramids and how they carefully preserved the bodies of their kings.

Established along the Nile, Egypt was blessed with ample natural resources. The Nile produced rich mud for pottery and bricks with plenty of fish and waterfowl, and the desert held precious metals and stone.[7] Egypt is also known for inventions such as paper and coloured ink, toothbrushes, toothpaste, and breath mints![8]

Agriculture was the backbone of Egypt, producing papyrus products, castor oil for lamps and medicinal purposes, flax for rope and clothing, and even beer made from emmer, a type of wheat grain.[9] Fed through a system of canals for irrigation, the Nile provided for plentiful crops that amply fed the Egyptians, with the rest stored in state-owned storehouses, either used for trade or kept for leaner years.[10] Joseph's story brings this concept to life. Are you starting to see the attraction of Egypt?

Egypt would not have been as charming without the Nile. The annual flooding of the Nile, producing fertile land as it receded, may have influenced the Egyptian sun god myth and other myths depicting the giving of life.[11] Along with her agricultural and spiritual significance, the Nile was a critical trade route for Egypt and the surrounding nations.[12] When God turned her to blood, we are talking about a major economic blow! This massive river is around 6,600 kilometres in length (4,100 miles).[13] Imagine the impact of this bloodied trade route from Egypt to the world.

Captivated by the Past

What interests me even more than Egypt's success is how her culture still charms people today. Her advanced civilisation and awe-inspiring architecture fascinate us. Amongst all the ancient cultures to have dominated the world's history stage, Egypt continues to hold a place in the Western world's modern art, including our movies, décor, and even our spirituality.

The Art Deco movement of the 1930s saw much influence from the Egyptian archaeological digs that occurred in the early twentieth century. Sleek cats graced mantels, and jewelled collars graced the necks of those who could afford them. We have created movies and TV shows about mummies, curses, and hidden Egyptian treasures.

So think about this—if Egypt and her culture still fascinate us, how much more might the shepherd people of Moses' day have been affected? When I compare their simple lives with Egypt's sophistication, I can imagine why they 'looked back' to Egypt, despite the horrors they experienced. The Egypt they lived in was a place of abundance, power, and structure. When the Israelites succumbed to depression and felt oppressed in the wilderness, they remembered the meat pots in Egypt and her plentiful crops of melons and cucumbers (Numbers 11). As long as the Nile River existed, Egypt had plenty of food!

Sadly, the Egyptian gods plagued the children of Israel long after their rescue. We are no different. Sometimes we are shackled to our past, despite leaving our harsh masters. Our baggage may be more than disappointments and personal sins. It may involve trauma and pain that act like a spiritual bungee cord pulling us back to the past we escaped from. Jacob's descendants had grown up and multiplied in Egypt. During their wilderness wanderings, they had to learn their real identity.

Ultimately, the Exodus story is a story of god against God. It is the story of sound defeat and humiliation. This is the outcome when God Almighty comes against the world's gods. That He cannot be defeated is a sound and eternal principle. From the Red Sea to the cross, the God of Israel stands and remains victorious.

Having disarmed principalities and powers, He made a public spectacle of them, triumphing over them in it. (Colossians 2:15).

Later in our story, when God judged Pharaoh for refusing to let his people go, He directly aimed his blows at the Nile River and the sun. He showed Pharaoh and any who would listen that He is the God of creation. Their agricultural success was not the result of worshipping gods that protected the elements. It resulted from a good God who created the elements for our abundance.

Ultimately, the Exodus story is a story of god against God.

The story of Israel and her exodus from Egypt and entrance into her land is a historical event. It also reveals *our* story. God reveals in Scripture a story we can trust and learn from. We can believe God's words to Israel were true. And they remain true today. This gives us confidence in how we interpret both our faith journey and the new covenant written in Jesus' blood.

Personally, I am fascinated by the story of Israel. You can't make this stuff up! It is a story of hope, courage, victory, bitterness, mistakes, disappointment, rebellion, and a God who never gave up on a stiff-necked people, because He called them His own. He hasn't changed His mind. And truth be told, perhaps I recognise a bit of myself in the story.

As we journey with the Israelites from captivity to victory, I'd encourage you to remember how a strong culture overshadows a weaker one. Unless we firmly anchor to the culture of God's kingdom and refuse to be swallowed up by it, the surrounding culture will become our own. God's kingdom is a counter-culture to the kingdom of darkness, no matter the 'pharaoh' of the day. As people of promise, our kingdom culture is the real powerhouse. We just need eyes to see and faith to believe. The story of the Israelites helps us to understand our own fragility and weakness. And to humbly accept the grace God extends to us in Jesus.

3

How Did We Get Here?

Have you ever arrived at a point in your life where you abruptly stopped and wondered, 'How on earth did I get here?' I had one of these unsettling experiences, and it wasn't pleasant. Many years ago, after a period of extreme striving and surviving, I collapsed in a heap of fatigue and grey cloud. I couldn't understand the context I lived in anymore. I had been going so fast through my life that when my situation abruptly changed, I could not relate to my environment any longer. Who was I, and what was I doing? These moments are challenging, but sometimes they are necessary for us to recognise we are not fulfilling our destiny, and it is time for us to move on.

Egypt was a place of transition for Abraham's descendants, not a permanent home. The blessings God promised to Abraham began to multiply in Jacob's lifetime and especially through Joseph, Jacob's much loved younger son. God miraculously intervened in the lives of Jacob and his descendants by positioning Joseph in the pharaoh's court to provide food during a severe famine.

A Snatched Inheritance

We read more about Abraham's tenacious grandson, Jacob, than we do about his own son Isaac. Isaac had twins, Esau and Jacob. Jacob's life had many struggles, but his tenacity is an inspiring attribute. How would you like to go down in history as the one who dared to wrestle with God? Jacob formally became Israel when God changed his name, just as He had done for his grandfather (Genesis 32:28). The name change gave him a new identity. He went from Jacob, the one who grasped for his brother's position, to Israel, the one who contended with God and man. In making a nation, God sought one who would go after his inheritance. God blessed Jacob for chasing down the dreams He had placed in his heart.

Jacob knew how to snatch and run! In taking his brother's birthright, he took advantage of Esau's fleshly weakness. When he snatched the blessing associated with the birthright, he did so by deceit and left town before Esau could kill him (Genesis 27). But he began to learn how to stand and fight for what was his. So when Jacob's employer and relative, Laban, deceived him and gave him the wrong daughter in marriage, Jacob confronted Laban and made him promise to give him his rightful wife (Genesis 29). Two wives and eleven sons later, Jacob meets God in a wrestling match. Just like he grasped for his brother's position and blessing, he refused to let go until he received a blessing from God (Genesis 32:26).

Are we as tenacious in snatching our birthright back from the enemy of our souls? How much do we want the position God has for us? Through Jacob's tenacity and raw faith, we have the amazing story of Joseph and the early Egyptian years.

The Good Years

Jacob was blessed with possessions but had no substantial land to call his own. As a shepherd and livestock owner, he was a tent dweller, like his father and grandfather before him. But we see the beginnings of Promise with twelve healthy male descendants. Given Grandfather Abraham's slow start, this was impressive! Jacob's tribe was almost reduced to eleven because of some serious jealousy in the camp, but God had a rescue ready for young Joseph. Seventeen-year-old Joseph heard from God profoundly. But his family tired of his prophetic utterances, and he quickly lost brotherly relationships (Genesis 37). In fact, it was so bad, his brothers made a plan to kill him. God caused Joseph's elder brothers, Reuben and Judah, to intervene.

Instead of killing the young dreamer, the brothers sold him as a slave to passing traders. Joseph held fast to God's word during this troublesome time, while he also endured falsified charges of adultery that landed him in a dungeon cell. God used this time in Joseph's life to hone his spiritual gifts as he also grew in maturity.

Fast-forward thirteen years, and this young prophet of God is dressed in finery in the courts of Egypt, advising the king's rulers and trusted implicitly by Pharaoh himself. (Here's a lesson in not despising the word of the Lord. Sometimes it has small and even irritating beginnings. Sometimes it comes from the mouths of children—and has even been delivered through a donkey!)

Years later, when reunited with his treacherous brothers in Egypt, Joseph says to them:

> *I am your brother Joseph, whom you sold into Egypt. Now do not be grieved or angry with yourselves because you sold me here, for God sent me ahead of you to save lives… God sent me ahead of you to ensure for you a remnant on the earth, and to keep you alive by a great deliverance.* (Genesis 45:4–7 NASB)

Despite the horror his brothers put him through, Joseph had the revelation of a bigger picture. God sent him ahead of his family to save them and many others. And because of his prestigious position, the

Egyptians welcomed his family and gave them a bountiful living in the region of Goshen. This arrangement allowed them to keep and raise the herds they relied on for their sustenance and provision. At the outset, it appeared to be set up for a positive Egyptian stay.

We need to determine the seasons for camping and the seasons for moving on.

But God had revealed to Abraham there would be a dark period in his descendants' future (Genesis 15). The reality is that God orchestrated the Egyptian stay. Egypt wasn't the land God promised the descendants of Abraham, but it was necessary for a time. I wonder, however, if they would ever have arrived at their promised destination if the situation in Egypt hadn't changed?

What life circumstances cause us to become accustomed to the surrounding comforts that prevent us from chasing our future and the promises God has for us? What may have caused you personally to settle? We need to determine the seasons for camping and the seasons for moving on.

The Pain of the World

While Egypt is a geographical location, Egypt in Scripture can also represent the world. So, the Israelites' story is also one of removing them from the world and relocating them to a kingdom ruled by God. It is good to seek the patterns in Scripture because they show us sound spiritual principles we can trust.

Every human starts out 'in the world.' The heartbreaking story of Adam and Eve reveals them moving from promise, that place of beauty and safety we know as Eden, to the world. The world brought them heartache and provided no long-term solace. From this point forward, all of humanity—that means you and me, start out in the world's kingdom ruled and dominated by the prince of the power of the air (Ephesians 2:2).

Spiritually, 'the world' is ruled by Satan. This world is not geographical. It is a spiritual realm where the enemy of our souls governs in fear, deceit, greed, hopelessness, and every form of oppression and evil. It is this world God loved and sent His Son to. The Son of God came against the prince of the power of the air and defeated him soundly. While we walk on planet Earth and interact physically with it, this place is not our spiritual home.

In our spiritual journey, God relocates us from the enemy kingdom to His kingdom, releasing us from captivity into freedom. Our physical presence remains on Earth, but Scripture declares we sit in heavenly places spiritually (Ephesians 2:6) when we put our trust in God's Son.

Sentiment Changes

After Joseph's death, a pharaoh rose to power who hadn't known him. Perhaps if he knew of the esteemed Joseph, he would have esteemed Joseph's people. Even a cursory reading of how Egyptians viewed non-Egyptians may suggest why Joseph was unknown. It is possible the history of a Hebrew vizier,[1] Joseph's likely title, went unrecorded or was erased from Egyptian records. Even with Joseph's high status, he could not dine with the Egyptians because they considered dining with Hebrews to be an abomination (Genesis 43:32). What an absurd situation! But it was part of God's plan to force the Egyptians to submit to Joseph as master of their storehouses because they needed to eat.

There came a time when the Hebrews would have realised they were no longer welcome strangers in Egypt. Eventually, they became slaves. The protection and influence from the time of Joseph had well and truly ended, and captivity became their lot. Where to turn?

We arrive at a pivotal point in the Israelites' story. They are no longer one family but a substantial people group. While they were not yet a nation in the legitimate sense, they were definitely a nation in the making—they just needed to find their legs and their land.

In our spiritual journey, God relocates us from the enemy kingdom to His kingdom, releasing us from captivity into freedom.

God's blessing and the Promise of a multitude of descendants *is* being fulfilled. The humble beginning of just one son of Promise to Abraham has become a fruitful people group. Sadly, the pharaoh of the day did not appreciate the prophetic outcome of 'exceedingly fruitful' humans during his rule. This is the pharaoh of Moses' early story—a cold-blooded killer with a heart of stone, intent on forcing population control of the Hebrew family group.

After four hundred plus years under Egyptian rule, God now reveals His hand. It's time for a rescue.

4

Enemy Tactics

The story of the Israelites' captivity is one of extreme oppression, hatred, jealousy, and even murderous intent. This is always what the enemy has planned for God's children, whether of ancient Israelite heritage or those grafted into the family through Jesus. The enemy would have been very aware of the promises God gave to Abraham's people, and he knew about the promised Seed; the ultimate rescue plan we know as the Son of God.

> *And I will put enmity between you and the woman, and between your seed and her Seed; He shall bruise your head, and you shall bruise His heel. (Genesis 3:15)*

Throughout the story, the enemy was laying down his plans in opposition to God's plans. But in time, God redeemed the dungeon years for Joseph, and the years of captivity birthed a promised nation. The God of Abraham, Isaac, and Jacob was still at work. When times are tough, remember our God works all things together for good, for the people who love Him and are called according to His purpose (Romans 8:28).

Despite the difficulties, the story of Moses should encourage us...

Birthing a Rescue

When a new pharaoh saw how the Hebrew people multiplied, he decreed all Hebrew baby boys were to be put to death at birth and commanded the Hebrew midwives to carry out his orders. These courageous women refused, fearing God over pharaoh (Exodus 1).

Amidst this chaos and brutality, a little boy arrived to parents, Amram and Jochebed, of the tribe of Levi. I don't know how much they knew of their God at this point in their story, as it would appear they hadn't yet had a personal encounter. But by faith, they hid their beautiful little boy and waited on God for deliverance (Hebrews 11:23). These parents were certainly not about to listen to Pharaoh's death decree or to the enemy's plans laid out for their newborn son.

Faith doesn't look sophisticated. It looks like a couple in a house in Goshen, oppressed by the enemy every day and choosing to press into the generational stories of a God who made a promise to their fathers. It looks like two Hebrew midwives who choose to fear God over man and refuse to have innocent blood on their hands. Let's pray for the heart of these midwives as *we* move through enemy territory and navigate the terrain. Are we also courageous enough to trust God with our loved ones and with the hopes and dreams of our hearts, trusting God Almighty when everything around us is screaming the decree of the enemy?

Through their faith and God's miraculous intervention, the child Moses grew up under the protection of Pharaoh's daughter in Egypt's royal courts. Like Joseph, he was saved from death and planted in a position of influence to protect the children of God, keeping God's Promise to Abraham alive. After the encounter at the burning bush, Moses was designated as God's Prophet to the nation he was birthing right under Pharaoh's nose.

But Moses' first interaction with Pharaoh as God's Prophet doesn't go well for the people. Instead of being released as Moses told them would happen, Pharaoh subjected them to even harder labour. Moses had received a divine command at the burning bush to rescue God's people, which left Moses doubting his calling (Exodus 5:22–23). When we step into the plans God has for us, we may find ourselves in the enemy's cross-hairs. This is the time to press in and remember God's promises spoken before His enemy had anything to say. The enemy will come against the children of God. But God's plans will always outdo the enemy's attempts at diversion, discouragement, and delay.

Delay Tactics!

I see distinct similarities in the story of Israel's captivity and release with how the enemy operates today. Persecution intensified right before God's rescue. We see the enemy's tactic of overt and unfair punishment, which is designed to stop God's work in our lives.

The brick quota for the Hebrew slaves was already being met under extreme duress. When Moses challenged Pharaoh and requested leave to worship God, Pharaoh stiffened his chin and stopped providing straw to the Hebrews to make the bricks. They now had to collect the straw themselves. However, he did not reduce their quota of bricks. Pharaoh declared it was their idleness that caused them to request leave from their duties to sacrifice to their God. Further, his overt punishment was designed to stop them from listening to what he called 'false words' (Exodus 5:9). Pharaoh openly denied the word of God that was delivered through His prophets and declared it to be untrue.

Unfortunately, the punishment worked. The Israelites became angry with the prophet of God, who had stirred up this trouble for them. Isn't that just like the enemy? He lies, steals, and brings destruction, and then audaciously blames God's people and His word. This is clearly not a new tactic! Breakthrough was around the corner, but the people could only focus on their pain and on trying to reduce it—or at the very least, to bear it.

> *When we step into the plans God has for us, we may find ourselves in the enemy's cross-hairs.*

Consider the following enemy tactics used in Exodus chapter 5. Do any of these sound familiar?

1. Strong accusations, taunting, and blame.

2. Load them up with work and exhaust them.

3. Create a situation where they cannot meet requirements.

4. Punish them for being unable to meet the impossible standards.

5. Create fear of punishment and use unjust punishment to 'whip up' the fear (i.e., when the people realise they cannot please their bondage masters).

6. Oppress the people to get them to blame their leaders or God.

7. Convince them God is not telling them the truth, and that He won't come through. Bring this about by making the situation appear impossible.

8. Bring division between the people. The Hebrew foremen placed strong blame on Moses and Aaron; 'May the LORD judge and punish you for making us stink before Pharaoh and his officials' (Exodus 5:21 NLT).

If we are honest, we have probably succumbed to one or more of these enemy tactics, too. Notice that Pharaoh's response was multi-pronged. He didn't use just one tactic. The enemy is strategic in his approach, endeavouring to inflict as much damage as possible. It is difficult amid chaos to see through the smoke screen to the actual attack. We are too busy trying to protect ourselves and our loved ones, or maybe we have taken shrapnel and have ceased to function normally. It requires a strong faith shield against the enemy's fiery arrows (Ephesians 6:16).

Holding Our Position

The enemy's tactic to tie people up in so much work they don't have time to worship or spend time with God is in operation today! Without the power of relationship and praise in our lives, we become weak. That's exactly where the enemy wants us, and he is exceptionally practised at targeting human vulnerabilities. He wants us out of action. Did you know he hates it when the saints praise their God? He'd much rather hear us complaining. According to the Acts 16 story of Paul and Silas, praise *literally* breaks chains. We don't just sing about chain-breaking because it sounds good. Praise is a powerful spiritual principle for deliverance and one God has provided to us as a weapon against the enemy's tactics. The more the enemy rants, the stronger our praise should be. When we praise, we raise God up over our enemy, declaring Him bigger than the enemy and his tricks.

There are many enemy tactics designed to delay God's promises from being fulfilled in our lives and cause us to fear He will not answer us. God's great generals of the faith were not immune to the devil's ploy. Daniel received a vision that grieved him, causing him to mourn for three full weeks. It was at the conclusion of this period an angel helped Daniel understand what was occurring in the supernatural realm. From Daniel's perspective, there was a full three weeks of mourning and grief in his spirit as he tried to process the enormity of the message he had received. But in the spiritual realm, an actual battle was taking place (Daniel 10). Daniel had not been forgotten, nor was God trying to test his faith or patience. Daniel was experiencing a dark night of the soul while the enemy waged war against the angelic messenger of God sent to bring Daniel a measure of strength and comfort.

> *But, beloved, do not forget this one thing, that with the Lord one day is as a thousand years, and a thousand years as one day. The Lord is not slack concerning His promise, as some count slackness, but is longsuffering toward us, not willing that any should perish but that all should come to repentance.* (2 Peter 3:8–9)

We do not have to succumb to the enemy's plans for us. Like Daniel, we may have to battle it out a bit and literally wait for the Lord's answer. We must remember we don't fight in the natural (Ephesians 6), and Jesus has already provided the victory over our enemy (Colossians 2:15). Sometimes we must step into that victory and hold our place. I'm telling you now, it's not comfortable, nor easy! We have this short story of Daniel and the long story of Job to give us insight into how much trouble the enemy can cause the saints. But the victory is complete and available. Yes, we have to walk it out, but don't let the enemy deceive you into believing he has the final say. He will try to wear you out and cause you to give up. Faith perseveres.

When we praise, we raise God up over our enemy, declaring Him bigger than the enemy and his tricks.

Despite the pain and delay, Israel was forming in the womb of Egypt. She would need to trust her God and get to know His ways after so many years under the influence of the Egyptians and their gods. She needed to learn about her God before beginning her significant journey as a torchbearer for the coming Messiah. He was the One to empower her unique calling.

Behind the Scenes

The enemy of our souls is the one who designed the worship behind the gods of Egypt and engineered the captivity and mistreatment of the Hebrews. He is the one, along with the principalities, powers, rulers of darkness, and spiritual hosts of wickedness (Ephesians 6), behind every counterfeit and proud government that sets itself up against the Most High God. Egypt was no exception. In fact, she founded much of the occult worship and false religion still present in the world today. Behind the power of the pyramids and the magic symbols lies the serpent of old. The enemy's complex web is not complex to God Almighty, who sees all. The created beings worshipped by the Egyptians were not the animals depicted in murals, headwear, and tombs. They were an all-star cast; the 'stars of heaven' referred to in Revelation:

> *His tail drew a third of the stars of heaven and threw them to the earth. And the dragon stood before the woman who was ready to give birth, to devour her Child as soon as it was born.* (Revelation 12:4)

I don't think this revelatory picture is a one-time event. This picture speaks of the devil who repeatedly persecuted Israel and slaughtered her male children. He orchestrated these monstrous plans to derail the Promise and prevent the Messiah's birth. This dragon of Revelation enticed Pharaoh to kill the newborn boys in the time of Moses. He repeated this strategy through Herod when he found out a Jewish king had been born.

On both occasions, there was a saviour in the making. The first was Moses, a saviour in the natural world and a major and powerful prophet, who God raised up to birth Israel as a nation. The second was the much-awaited Seed, prophesied way back in Genesis and the Saviour of the world, who we now know as Jesus (Yeshua). This Saviour would provide the ultimate sacrifice for the children of Israel and would add other nations to God's inheritance. He would also destroy the devil's power and make a way for humankind to be set free from his tyranny. This explains why the devil went to the lengths he did.

The Final Say

You really can do all things through Christ, who strengthens you if you submit to the Spirit of God. God has not given us scripts to read and follow. He gave us the actual person of Jesus in spirit form to live out these victories in us. Sometimes it seems the biggest battle we face as believers is not the immediate issue we are walking through; it's the act of yielding to the Spirit of God! Isn't that the truth? Is it any wonder the enemy speaks out against God? He doesn't want us to realise the power we have when we surrender our limited resources and understanding to the unlimited resources and power of the mighty God, who formed a nation from an old man and an old woman who couldn't have children.

> *For every child of God defeats this evil world, and we achieve this victory through our faith. And who can win this battle against the world? Only those who believe that Jesus is the Son of God.* (1 John 5:4–5 NLT)

5

God's Children in Bondage?

Today, millions of people do not realise they are in spiritual captivity, being yoked to the enemy as he drapes a controlling arm around their shoulders and whispers false promises in their ears. The children of Israel strongly felt the whip of the enemy and the back-breaking labour of their servitude. We have here a literal picture of what bondage looks like. The whip of the Egyptians was a daily reality, and the Hebrew slaves bore the marks of such treatment.

Many hide away with their souls in torment while outwardly presenting a big smile and not a mark to be seen. The spiritual reality of bondage (or captivity) is profound and heartbreaking, just as much as it was in the days of Moses. It was not the Lord who brought the captivity, but it *was* the Lord who broke the arm of the bondage maker and set the captives free.

For many, bondage is 'just the way it is'. If you don't know there's a better life, you won't know to seek it. The enemy of our souls works overtime to hide his plans and the counterfeits he lures people with. When you don't even believe there is a God to save you, how deeply dark must that bondage feel?

Believers in Captivity

As believers in Jesus, we can have a part of our soul still in captivity, whether to fear, bitterness, discouragement, or any other burden we have yet to lay down. These access points allow the enemy into our lives. This is one reason why we need the work of the Spirit to renew us completely—to make us new, transforming us from the inside out, beginning with our minds (Romans 12:2).

It is better to hand over our hurts, disappointments, and pain to God and let Him deal with them than to carry the bitter burden that slowly destroys us from the inside out.

Much like a continual improvement program in the business world, we need to surrender to the process of being upgraded, honed, and refined. We cannot afford to leave *any* part of us unprotected by refusing or limiting the renewing work of the Spirit. When even a small part of us remains unrenewed, we can give the enemy a right to put spiritual chains on us in that area. Remember, he prowls around looking for an opportunity to say, 'Gotcha!'

Consider, for example, the heavy chains of unforgiveness. God warns us most clearly in Scripture to forgive freely in the same manner He forgives us of our many sins. When we choose to keep the anger, hurt, pain, and judgement in our hearts, we give the enemy rights. I liken our soul to a piece of land. We need to ensure the land does not have any place for squatters to move in! Once they are in, they are very difficult to move. It is better to hand over our hurts, disappointments, and pain to God and let Him deal with them, than to carry the bitter burden that slowly destroys us from the inside out.

Remember the straw and bricks from the previous chapter? The enemy persecuted God's people to *prevent them* from worshipping God. He would not *release* them to worship because we find freedom from our chains in worship. Let me tell you a story to illustrate this point.

The Lord gave me an unusual mental picture during a worship meeting one evening. I saw a believer I know trying to physically get closer to other worshippers, but he was prevented from doing so because of a ball and chain around his ankle. When he tried to move closer to the group, he stumbled and fell. It was confronting. In this picture, the ball and chain were not representative of someone still bound by the world. So what did it represent?

In years gone by, the ball and chain were applied to prisoners to keep them from escaping and limit their movement within a tight boundary. The spiritual reality of believers in shackles *is* confronting, particularly if this is a new concept for you. But the enemy will keep us in an area of captivity for as long as we are ignorant of it. In this illustration, Satan did not want this man to join in worship or get close to the fellowship of believers. He knew this would mean a breakthrough. This also illustrates that Satan doesn't mind you going to church. He just doesn't want you experiencing the Spirit's power.

There is an exciting truth in God's word:

He has sent me to comfort the brokenhearted and to proclaim that captives will be released and prisoners will be freed. (Isaiah 61:1NLT)

I have read this verse many times, but I recently saw the distinction between captive and prisoner. A prisoner is under punishment for breaking the law. They have usually been locked away to do time under the administration of a warden in a judicial system. A captive is someone being held against their will. A captive is not necessarily a prisoner. When you are saved through the grace and work of Jesus, you are not a prisoner anymore. But... you can remain captive in certain areas of your life.

You do not have to stay shackled to the past.

You can remain captive to the past, to trauma, to greed, to certain sins, etc. We can also allow the enemy access to our lives once we have been saved. He won't hesitate to shackle us in that area, such as fear, confusion, disappointment, deep and prolonged grief, lust, and many more.

Sometimes the damage is done when we are very young, and a part of us cannot develop or grow normally. This is the case with children who have experienced deep trauma. It is the work of Jesus to heal the broken-hearted (Isaiah 61:1). You do not have to stay shackled to the past, to trauma, sins, or any emotional pain or baggage you carry.

Please know the enemy does not play fair! Any chance he gets to mess up your life, he will take (and I speak from experience!). This is why believers in Jesus are called to be vigilant. We need to learn to fight for our freedom and not accept enemy propaganda.

Praise God Jesus holds the key to our release in these shackled areas! Jesus accomplished His mission and provided an answer for all kinds of spiritual and natural captivity. It is the work of the Spirit to renew us into the image of Jesus. God created people in *His* image, and His desire is always for our freedom.

> *He is so rich in kindness and grace that he purchased our freedom with the blood of his Son and forgave our sins.* (Ephesians 1:7 NLT)

The Whip of Religion

Egyptian whips on the backs of the Hebrew slaves brought fear and intimidation, punishment, and physical pain. The whip of religion will do no less. It's a much-used whip. Sadly, many use it to flagellate themselves under the guilt of their own wrongdoing and condemnation. The whip of religion is the control of one's conscience, spiritual disciplines, and beliefs. Spiritual dictators have used it with much success over millennia to oppress the God-given spiritual fruit of people under their supposed 'care.' Religion operates in many contexts. Don't confuse religion with faith or with the God of the Bible; religion is about control.

The very religious Egyptians were intent on serving their gods and their supposedly semi-divine Pharaoh by creating temples, monuments, and cities. Religion always tries to build its own temple. Religion is a spirit—many spirits, in fact, but we define the religious spirit as a particular type.

The spirit of religion imposes control over people created with a free will to choose God. This spirit is hideous! Its most used words include don't, can't, guilt, fear, shame, blame, and judgement (the whip). The spirit prevents people from seeing God's truth by trapping them in the religious web of guilt, fear, and the need to do the works that supposedly prevent great judgement. It uses ritual, tradition, symbolism, and uniform to give the impression of a spiritual superiority, which encourages the masses in their ignorance to bow to their higher plane of spirituality. It sets itself up against the knowledge of God and especially the work of the Spirit because it cannot control the work of the Spirit and knows people are set free by it! Keep them in pews, temples, on spiritual pilgrimages, and tied up in vows and ritual observance—but under no circumstance let them experience the Spirit of God. Why? He is the chain breaker. (Religion likes to keep its prisoners.)

When you experience the power of the Spirit of God and the freedom He brings, you flee from your bondage masters. Not only that, but you tell others about their dictatorship and foul lies. The spirit of religion sets itself up directly in opposition to God. Beware! It particularly likes to set itself up in churches and quote from the Bible. It rarely speaks of personal or revelatory experience (it doesn't have any). It usually looks very well kept from the outside, with an extra-large Bible in hand and a pew with its name on it. It will arc up at any change that threatens its status quo and absolutely abhors free worship!

When you experience the power of the Spirit of God and the freedom He brings, you flee from your bondage masters.

Religion says, 'Keep to the script, people, don't look up, and don't stop. Baptise only this way. Take communion only that way. Keep the coffee pot on hot and make sure the carpets are regularly cleaned. If you don't, I'll… (insert any threat you like here)'. I recognise this spirit well. It loves to keep you busy, so you can't hear the still, small voice of God. Praise God, He set me free from its continual barrage of lies in my spiritual ears.

The whip can kill…

Being flogged is a brutal and humiliating punishment that has killed people. Spiritually, the whip is a symbol of control. Its intention is to threaten people into conforming to a system of rules, and it enforces obedience. If you are likely to receive punishment for a difference in action or opinion, you will tend to follow the rules. If the fear of what could happen to your soul if you don't follow the rules plagues you, you will surely follow them.

God has His regulations to protect His people from the consequences of sin, but He allows free will. Religion has rules for the subjection of people to keep them from experiencing freedom, and it crushes free will.

The power of religion will bring death. It has no life in its system, being birthed from hell as a counterfeit to God-ordained laws and requirements. If you remain under the whip of religion, you will die a slow spiritual death. One stinging outcome of a religious whip is your struggle to approach Father God because of your deep shame. Jesus was flogged before His crucifixion. He has already taken your flogging—and the deep shame of knowing your sin. Get to know Jesus, and you can put your whip down.

Understand the pull of religion is strong and often subtle. Paul had to remind the esteemed and anointed Apostle Peter about the pull of religion as he caught Peter submitting to its power. Peter did not want to look bad in front of a visiting Jewish group who held some sway (Galatians 2:11–21). This is a challenging passage because Peter has experienced the power of the Spirit at this point in his life. I carefully point out that, for a moment, a force that had expectations of how he would behave as a Jew cowed him. Paul reminds him quickly that to eat with non-Jews (Gentiles) in freedom one day, and then to withdraw from them while the Jewish visitors were present, was nothing short of hypocrisy. It was a powerful force, though, with the righteous Barnabas eventually succumbing.

Under the old covenant, there was a separation between Jews and others according to the regulations of holiness. For example, an uncircumcised non-Jew could not partake of Passover. Now, under the new covenant, Peter and company are put into the spotlight. Will they listen to the word of the Lord regarding who is clean and who isn't? Learning the truth of the word of God is the first step. Asking for and applying the Holy Spirit's discernment is necessary to interpret and apply the word *correctly*.

Standing up against religion and recognising it can be difficult, especially when the issue is biblical. Sometimes we are in danger of using the old Christian proof-text to make our case without having knowledge of the true meaning or the context. Religion says, 'This is right, and that is wrong!' (interpreted as 'I am right and you are wrong'). The Spirit of God brings a heart check and a love for truth *and* people. The Spirit brings revelation, and His sound is the sound of wisdom.

I have one last point on the whip of religion. If you have come out from underneath it, do not put yourself back under it! That is like inviting the warden for a cup of tea.

A Prison-breaking God

Isaiah tells us the Seed of Abraham (Jesus the Messiah) came to set captives free:

He has sent Me to heal the brokenhearted, to proclaim liberty to the captives, and the opening of the prison to those who are bound... (Isaiah 61:1).

Let's not miss this beautiful truth! The God of the Israelites is the same today. He has not changed. In fact, we read the story of the Israelites to see who *our* God is. We learn about Him through His attributes and what He says and does. When we think of Jesus in terms of Saviour, I wonder if we include the concept of the One who breaks down prison doors and heals broken hearts.

The gospel message is a complete rescue.

A quick study of the word Saviour helps to strengthen our understanding of what Jesus did on the cross and continues to do today. The Greek word for Saviour, found in at least Luke, John, and Acts, is *sótér*. A little background check reveals sótér, as a proper noun, is 'Jesus Christ who saves believers from their sins *and delivers them into His safety*'.[1] Wow! Jesus Christ saves us from our sins AND delivers us into His safety. This is a powerful statement of being relocated into a new realm—a new kingdom of Jesus' presence. The God who saves is the God who lives with us, just as He lived with the children of Israel in days of old.

Please understand this! The gospel message is a complete rescue—not a partial rescue. Saviour includes the concepts of being rescued from one's sin, brought into the presence of God, delivered from one's enemies, and healed by the power of the living God. It includes provision and purpose. God did not simply order the Israelites out of the land of Egypt and tell them, 'You're free!' He orchestrated a salvation plan that stretched from Abraham to Joshua and beyond. This prison-breaking, unchanging God is the same for you today.

There is a partial gospel message denying Jesus His true power. It has denied many their inheritance. It may allow you to be 'saved' only to the point of having your sins forgiven so you can trip over the threshold of heaven with a tremendous sigh of relief once your time on Earth is done.

What about the gospel of 'I hope I will go to heaven when I die?' Many who claim to believe in Jesus are still in captivity in their minds and hearts, which can also translate to their physical bodies (e.g., anxiety, depression, bitterness, etc.). Jesus is not a partial Saviour. He saves absolutely, and He calls us to believe in all His works, despite our understanding or life experiences. If we do not believe in the full work of Jesus, we live in partial belief.

This prison-breaking, unchanging God is the same for you today.

Paul refers soberly to a gospel that is not actually the gospel of Christ (Galatians 1). Any version of the gospel that strips Jesus of His power has twisted the true gospel. It is entirely possible for a good, loving, well-intentioned believer of Jesus to believe a partial gospel. I know this for a fact. I was one of them.

It is the Lord's work and His pattern in Scripture to take us out of the world and into His kingdom. We cannot find our fulfilment in the world. Ironically and tragically, the land of Promise was the place of captivity when Jesus arrived on Earth. We can hand over our promise, and the enemy won't wait for a second chance to bring us back into his kingdom.

Our Lighthouse

The light of Jesus is not only a concept; it's a tangible substance we can apply to those dark recesses of our souls where the clean-up needs to happen. How many of us have a spare room? What goes on in that spare room is not usually on open display for visitors, right? And who would even consider entering the scary spare room without turning on the light? In the light, you find treasures you forgot you had! And also, in the light, you may find boxes and items varying from unsorted to unsavoury! Our heart has many rooms, and it is easy to close the door on those 'not for visitors' areas. But the Holy Spirit is not a visitor, and He already knows what happens in the dark…

The light of Jesus is powerful for exposing and enabling us to see with spiritual clarity. 'In Your light we see light!' (Psalm 36:9). Let the light separate you from the darkness and open those prison doors to set your captive free in all areas needing release. I pray for courage to let Jesus turn that light on!

6

Salvation Is at Hand

I had my spiritual rescue at a time I didn't realise I needed rescuing. Sometimes you just don't know you are in a form of captivity. Like the proverbial frog in the pot, the water keeps getting hotter, but you don't notice until it's too much to bear. In my story, I literally cried out one day, 'Somebody help me!' I did not cry out to God specifically. He was, however, the only one to answer me.

God heard their cries…

Now it happened in the process of time that the king of Egypt died. Then the children of Israel groaned because of the bondage, and they cried out; and their cry came up to God because of the bondage. So God heard their groaning, and God remembered His covenant with Abraham, with Isaac, and with Jacob. And God looked upon the children of Israel, and God acknowledged them. (Exodus 2:23–25)

A Saviour Figure

After Moses fled Egypt to Midian, he encountered God at the burning bush. The Lord tells him He has heard the cries of His people, and He has seen their oppression and knows their sorrow (Exodus 3). Note that God claims the Hebrews as 'My' people. It is time. Captivity is about to end. Moses just needs to get with God's program, despite needing some convincing. However, God had an opportunity Moses couldn't turn down. According to Stephen (Acts 7), there was a time when Moses thought he could do some good for his people. It appears he thought he could use his position as the adopted son of Pharaoh's daughter to gain relief from their oppression. But this time was now forty years in the past. Moses no longer believed he was the right candidate. As an eighty-year-old fugitive shepherd with a family to feed, what exactly could he do?

Like Joseph, God positioned Moses in the most unlikely manner. Joseph was sold and then plucked from prison to ascend to the immediate status of vizier over Pharaoh's affairs. Moses was hidden amongst the Nile reeds and plucked from its waters to safety by the daughter of the palace. His life would become interwoven with the courts of Pharaoh as he learned the Egyptians' ways. Neither Moses nor his parents would have known the importance of this tuition and life experience. Even at the burning bush, the light didn't dawn so easily on this Hebrew-Egyptian, turned shepherd.

I resonate with Moses! How many times has the Lord revealed something to me, and I have stared directly into His light but not understood the message (or maybe I was scared to hear it!)? When we look at Moses' story, we must see ourselves. We must see the fragility of the human but recognise the power available to the person who yields to God.

You cannot imagine the Israelites' story without the story of Moses. Moses was the man the Lord picked for the job of wilderness prophet. But, before Moses could lead God's children to the land of

Promise, he had to lead them out of captivity. Moses represents the Person of Jesus Christ. He was a strong leader, prophet, judge, and spiritual teacher who led in a time before Christ with a purpose of raising a nation that would birth the Light of the World. Moses was a saviour-type, presenting Christ to a people who did not yet know Him. Jesus was always the plan of God.

Moses is recorded as the humblest man on Earth (Numbers 12:3), which is why God could use him for the significant work of carrying a nation and mediating a covenant. Humility is the work of the Spirit. Like Jesus, Moses left his home and comforts to walk with broken and needy people and submitted his life to God to do this work.

We must see the fragility of the human but recognise the power available to the person who yields to God.

The Pain of Resistance

During the extended period of captivity, followed by the unusual period of the plagues and the hardening of Pharaoh's already hard heart, the people of Goshen hoped for their salvation. God fairly warned Pharaoh if he did not relinquish His firstborn (the Hebrews), then He would have to take Pharaoh's firstborn—a life for a life. Pharaoh was far too stubborn to listen. Therefore, God met Pharaoh where he was and waited until Pharaoh effectively said, 'I surrender!' Sometimes there is a painful process leading to salvation!

In the waiting, God worked powerfully. His children would know His protective hand while witnessing the destruction He would bring to Egypt. From these signs and wonders, Israel would come to know the God they were called to serve. They would recognise His powerful hand was not only coming against the arrogant Pharaoh, but it was coming down in judgement against Egypt's gods; those fallen ones who set themselves up in rebellion against the Most High God and demanded to be worshipped. As one plague ended and another began, the Egyptians also had ample opportunity to recognise the Almighty's power.

God started out gently. First, there was a polite request to let His people go, which Pharaoh denied (Exodus 5). Then, there was the miraculous sign of Aaron's rod becoming a snake. However, when the rod of Aaron swallowed up the magician's rods (Exodus 7), we see Pharaoh getting his back up and readying for a fight. He did not understand he was out-classed. This arrogant king really thought he could dictate terms to the God of Israel.

Initially, as Moses and Aaron went back and forth to Pharaoh announcing God's words and the subsequent plagues that would come, Pharaoh's magicians pulled off a counterfeit of God's signs and wonders. It is almost humorous to read how the magicians also produced bloodied water and frogs—adding to the plagues and punishments on their nation and its people! However, that's all they had. Like a limited party trick, their magic didn't even extend to the third plague of lice. In fairness to these magicians, when they could not produce any lice, they declared to Pharaoh, 'This is the finger of God' (Exodus 8:19)! Pharaoh refused to listen. It would have served him well to do so.

Here, we have a picture of a very stubborn, hard-hearted man who staunchly refused to listen to Moses and Aaron, to reason, or to the pleas of servants when they realised Egypt was being destroyed. God went to extraordinary lengths to extract His people. In this, He shows such mercy, which at first we may completely miss. God knows Pharaoh's heart and what Pharaoh will choose, but He does not go directly from small signs to the plague of death. With every plague, there is a punishment against Egypt, her pharaoh, and her gods. But there is also mercy for anyone willing to open their eyes. The people of Egypt needed God, too. They needed to learn that the gods of Egypt could not come close to His power and authority.

By the time the plague of large hail hit, some concerned servants of Pharaoh ran to secure their livestock and bring their servants indoors. Because of their actions, they saved their servants and livestock. These few were beginning to get the picture of Israel's God.

If he was so arrogant and wicked, why did God allow this pharaoh to rule? God provides us with the answer:

But indeed for this purpose I have raised you up, that I may show My power in you, and that My name may be declared in all the earth. (Exodus 9:16)

There is a bigger plan. It is God's will for everyone to know Him and be released from the bondage of their respective task-masters. God would reveal His signs and wonders in the land of false gods, and He would use them to bring judgement to Egypt and the release of His people (Exodus 7:3–5).

A Strategic Blow!

Dr Nicholas Schaser of Israel Bible Center says in our English Bible translations, we miss God's judgement on Egypt's gods, hidden in the eighth plague of locusts.[1] Where we read that locusts covered the *face* of the whole earth, the Hebrew reveals locusts covered the *eye* (ayin) of the land. This refers to the blotting out of the sun.[2] This passage, therefore, tells us Amun-Ra, the 'glorious' Egyptian sun god, was blinded! Not only that, but he was blinded by a ferocious blanket of insects. Now there's an insult.

When the deep, palpable darkness of the ninth plague fell on the land, the Egyptians surely knew their sun god, Amun-Ra, had been defeated. But why was this darkness so dark? God is the true source of light. Therefore, the absence of God is the absence of light. Even the sun bows before Him as a created thing. God made a declaration in this ninth plague there is *no* light in the Egyptians' gods. The power of God Almighty completely blinded the eye of Egypt. But protected in Goshen, the Hebrews had light in their homes (Exodus 10:23).

The first principle of creation is mirrored here—light separating from darkness. It is fitting that God visibly separated the Hebrews (God's children) from the Egyptians (the world) by the light in their homes. The God of Jesus Christ, who says He is the Light of the world, revealed His power and nature in this plague. Jesus calls *us* to be light today. God has separated us from the world by His light emanating from our lives.

Before the Hebrews could move from the land of captivity, God would execute His final judgement. Pharaoh had been fairly warned! He could have avoided this pain, but he lived in his own personal world of pride. This final plague of death would bring victory to God's people and destruction to Egypt. Only God Almighty is victorious over death.

Sometimes there is a painful process leading to salvation!

Pharaoh is a vessel by which the whole earth would understand Israel's God. Pharaoh's position provided the perfect global megaphone. Who wouldn't hear of the power of Egypt failing against the hand of the Hebrews' God? Imagine the merchants travelling to Egypt to trade and coming away in awe of the destruction and lack they witnessed. Word would have travelled far and wide. Not to mention that later in our story, a missing pharaoh will be difficult to explain… The Egyptians did not like to record their defeats,[3] so I imagine they came up with a suitable story that didn't involve humiliation at the hands of an unknown God and a Hebrew shepherd-prophet with a strange stick.

While the Hebrews would soon see their salvation, it would be many years before their spiritual night would turn to day. My journey also involved God's rescue in a practical way, releasing me from physical burdens before my spiritual eyes were ready for the light. In the dark period before dawn, we see a haze of light on the horizon but are unable to make out the dim shapes around us. But minute by minute, hour by hour, the light grows into a rosy glow, and suddenly, our surroundings develop clarity. As my light dawned, I learned to recognise and trust His voice and seek His signs in my life. And I learned He is for me, just like He was for the Israelites of old.

7

The Lessons of Passover

The Wholeness of the Lamb

It was during the early period of Covid-19 isolation I felt drawn to Passover. Besides this personal tug, there was much being said about the Passover of 2020 and its spiritual significance in light of global events. I re-read the story from Exodus 12. The culmination of all the plagues God released against Egypt was the death of Egypt's firstborn. After this plague, Pharaoh would release the Israelites. However, they had to follow God's explicit instructions to ensure their protection from the plague of death.

I saw a principle hidden within the Passover regulations we desperately need today. Each household had to cook its lamb whole and consume all of it at the meal. They were not to leave any lamb until the next day. I saw the requirement to partake of the *whole* lamb, which represented Jesus. I felt a strong call that while we hid inside our houses, we were to partake of the Lamb in His fullness—partaking in all He is and all He offers us. We were—and are, to partake of the whole Lamb, not just the parts we like or the parts that make sense to us. We are to feed our spiritual selves with *all* Jesus is, leaving nothing.

How many believers can say without hesitation they regularly partake of the whole Lamb of God? Why are we spiritually hungering, even in our churches? Why do we grow spiritually weary? Could it be that we are not partaking of the whole Lamb? The One who gave Himself completely, holding nothing back, is still wooing us today to partake of His goodness and to nourish our souls and our spirits from His complete offering.

> *Our wholeness is reliant on our willingness to take Jesus at His word and in His fullness.*

His provision includes *our* wholeness (Isaiah 53:5 NLT). Isn't that a stunning truth? It ties our wholeness into the reality of the wholeness of Jesus' sacrifice. His complete sacrifice has provided for our complete (holistic) healing. Let that sink in for a moment.

There are many spiritual consequences of not partaking of the fullness of Jesus. However, the names of Jesus provide us with a powerful clue.

- Do we partake of Him as Saviour, but not Lord?

- Do we accept He is Bread but not believe He is Healer anymore?

- Are there parts of the person of Jesus we find confronting or just don't understand?

The problem with not partaking of the whole Lamb is we do not become whole. Our wholeness is reliant on our willingness to take Jesus at His word and in His fullness.

The lamb is also for a household. The family eats and partakes together, and the lamb sustains and fortifies them. Practically, the Israelites had a long journey ahead of them, and I imagine there was a level of uncertainty mixed with their excitement. While the Passover has a primary and important spiritual meaning, we see the Lord also physically fortified His people before their exit from Egypt. He provides for us both physically and spiritually. He meets all our needs. This was not a long, drawn-out feast. This was an urgent and hastily consumed meal in a fully-dressed state, ready to (literally) run out the door (Exodus 12:11). We will only be ready for the next major event in our lives if we partake intentionally and fully of the Lamb of God.

The Blood of Protection

Egypt's disobedience brought about her judgement. Pharaoh directly disobeyed the word of the Lord, and he did so wilfully and on multiple occasions. Therefore, the wrath of God was provoked against Pharaoh and Egypt for their disobedience and because Pharaoh had unjustly taken the firstborn of God and enslaved him ('him' being the descendants of Jacob).

Over the course of the plagues, there is a process of Israel's separation from Egypt. When it was time to deliver the fifth plague, God informed Pharaoh through Moses and Aaron He would make a distinction between His people and Pharaoh's people (Exodus 9:4). The Hebrews in Goshen remained unharmed, while the Egyptians suffered the consequences of God's divine judgement. God protected all His people from the remaining plagues. However, when we arrive at the story of the final plague—death of the firstborn, the Hebrews must apply God's instruction within their households. There is something different about this plague. God's instruction is in the form of a promise with a condition.

In obedience, the people of Israel listened to God's word delivered through Moses and applied the blood of the household lamb to the doorway of their residences. The blood had to be applied to each doorpost and lintel (the top of the doorframe). In this manner, it marked the entry to each house. Once applied, the occupants of each house had to remain indoors until the following morning, staying 'under the blood.' Later, when the Lord established His sacrificial system, the people would learn it was the blood of the animal offerings that made atonement for their souls (Leviticus 17).

The power of the blood of Jesus is prophetically declared through the application of the blood of the Passover lamb on the doorframe of each Israelite house in Goshen. The doorway is the entry to our personal space and can also be a representation of the doorway to our hearts, that innermost part of us. This is the doorway at which Jesus stands and knocks (Revelation 3:20).

Is there a message for us today? Yes. Remain under the blood of Jesus! Walk in obedience to our Father's words, and maintain a clean heart. Repent of any known sins, even as a believer (don't give the enemy an opportunity, Ephesians 4:27). While the blood of Jesus poured out at the cross is a once-for-all sacrifice, continuing to sin *wilfully* will cause us to come out from God's protection and under His judgement (Hebrews 10:26–27).

We can relocate ourselves from an obedient and protected state through our hearts and actions in the same way the Israelites would have lost their protection had they wandered out during the night when Death passed over. They had to remain 'under the blood' and, by doing so, remain in obedience to God's word.

> *For the* LORD *will pass through to strike the Egyptians; and when He sees the blood on the lintel and on the two doorposts, the* LORD *will pass over the door and not allow the destroyer to come into your houses to strike you.* (Exodus 12:23)

Note the intent of this verse is for God to deliver punishment (judgement) to the Egyptians, who were in defiance of God's word. The wrath of God (His judgement against sin) was *not* for His children. When we are in Christ, His blood covers us, and God's wrath is not for us. This is a powerful truth also seen through the psalms of David. The judgement of God is for those living in disobedience to Him, not for those living in relationship with Him. When I came to the point of realising the judgement of God was not for me, it was an incredible relief! I am destined for relationship and family, as represented by the households of Israel, intimately partaking of the Passover meal together.

We are protected when we are 'under the blood.' The blood of Jesus atones for the sins of our soul, making us right with the Father (Hebrews 9). The wrath of God is no longer in our future as we enjoy the protection of relationship, dwelling in the secret place of the Most High (Psalm 91).

Passover Principles for Us

I can't do justice to the subject of Israel's deliverance without digging into the Passover. There is a logical flow to the Passover preparation and its regulations. Like everything God does, there is purpose and a spiritual dimension for us to explore. Remember, He is a gracious Father; He designed Passover and all its components for the children's good.

Get rid of all leaven

Leaven is a real and natural substance that causes bread to rise. We would be more familiar with the term yeast. Scripture uses leaven, or yeast, to represent sin. (There is nothing sinful about yeast itself!) To help people understand the concept of sin, God made an association with yeast and the sin that so easily spreads through our lives if we don't take care of it. On the fourteenth day of the Passover month before blood was applied to the doorposts, the people had to remove all leaven from each household. It couldn't be packed away. It had to go! We should recognise this powerful principle of repentance.

As unleavened bread is flat, we are to come to God in humility, with nothing raised in opposition to Him on the altar of our heart.

A repentant heart immediately precedes salvation and the work of the body and blood of Jesus in our lives. It is through repentance that we come to the cross. Putting away our sin is a part of the process of salvation. It doesn't mean we won't sin again, but it means we have made an intentional decision to remove the leaven in our lives. God was very strict on this requirement within the Passover observance. He continues to be very strict on this topic, as seen in the way Paul dealt with sin in the church. All the leaven needs to go!

We see in the Passover a clear link between removal of leaven, application of the blood, *and* deliverance. These three go together and in that order. If we put away our sin and there is atonement for it, we experience deliverance from the kingdom of darkness. If we are still experiencing degrees of bondage as believers, it is wise to investigate to see if we have sin lurking. Ultimately, sin is rebellion towards God's requirements. It can be overt or covert! The Holy Spirit is the One to do the exposing and the clean-up, and I can attest to His gentleness and love in the process. But, we must be willing and desire His work in us. Refusing to give up our pride, belief systems, and wrong ways of living will mean we *won't* experience the fullness of deliverance. Ultimately, this is our choice, but it has a nasty sting.

Sin and Jesus don't mix

The lamb of Passover represents the Lamb of God, so the bread to be eaten with the roasted lamb of Passover had to be unleavened. Here is a clear principle that we cannot partake of the Son of God while partaking of sin! Sin and Jesus do not mix. The holiness of a holy God requires that *we* take on His holiness. Holiness is His requirement, and we cannot ignore it. To partake of the wholeness of Jesus also means to come in humility before a holy and powerful God. As yeast puffs up bread, so does our sin reveal the puffed-up nature of pride in our lives. By partaking in sin while claiming to be God's children, we proudly proclaim we will come to the table of God on our terms—not His. Wow!

As unleavened bread is flat, we are to come to God in humility, with nothing raised in opposition to Him on the altar of our heart. Later, when the people built the Tabernacle in the wilderness from a heavenly plan, they created a table for the showbread. Jesus is the Bread of Life, and the showbread of the Tabernacle represented Him. The Son of God has no sin in Him. The unleavened bread at the Passover table and on the table in the Tabernacle represent Jesus in whom there is no sin. (Note that spiritually, He is both Lamb and Bread; our sacrifice for sin and our spiritual nourishment.)

Circumcision of the heart

While the physical circumcision of all males represented the covenant between God and Abraham's descendants, we should recognise the *principle* of circumcision is not just for the Jews![1] In Exodus 12, God is abundantly clear to Moses that if anyone outside the family of Israel desired to partake of Passover, they had to be physically circumcised in accordance with God's requirements for His people. Let's remember Passover was a prophetic message—a spiritual picture—in which all its components point to the Messiah, Jesus. The wonderful news for us today from this ancient story is God allowed *outsiders* to partake of His rescue feast! He is very clear He only has one law, and He will abide with whoever keeps His law, despite their heritage:

*One **law** shall be for the native-born and for the stranger who dwells among you.* (Exodus 12:49, emphasis mine)

This is a position of privilege, but contains a warning. God does not play favourites. He works according to His divine law. If we follow His requirements, which include humility of heart and coming to Him only through the work of Jesus, we can be certain of His welcome.

We avoid the issue of pride in our hearts through the process of spiritual circumcision, which is the 'cutting away' of our sinful nature to make way for the character of Jesus in our lives. Jeremiah tells us the heart of humans is deceitful (17:9). We need the Spirit of God to search our hearts and reveal our hidden motivations (17:10). It's about coming to God on His terms, not ours.

Bitter herbs

For the Israelites, the bitter herbs spoke of the bitterness of captivity. God did not ignore this reality when He ordained the Passover feast. Our sin also brings bitterness that only the Son of God can take away. And Passover reminds us of the pain of Jesus' suffering caused by our sin.

Sometimes, we, too, have to take bitter herbs along our faith journey. Suffering will come in our walk with Jesus on this Earth. We can view the bitter herbs as being taken *because* of the lamb—but they are also taken *with* the lamb! In Jesus, we have all we need for our faith journey, including its bitter parts.

> *If we follow His requirements, which include humility of heart and coming to Him only through the work of Jesus, we can be certain of His welcome.*

Are you ready?

Finally, we have the need for readiness. Obedience and readiness are linked. In our obedience, we follow God's leading and requirements. When we acknowledge Jesus as our Saviour, we need to become a follower. We must be ready to follow Him, or we will be left behind. A future dimension of this Passover reality is for us to prepare spiritually for the return of Christ. We cannot afford to be apathetic towards our ultimate day of deliverance.

Before God freed the Israelites from Egypt, He planned for them to partake of the wonder of salvation, according to the work of Christ. They did not yet know Him, but that didn't matter because Christ's sacrifice was in place before the foundation of the world (Revelation 13:8). Physically, this nation had not yet birthed its Messiah. Spiritually, its Messiah was making Himself known. He also knew they needed hope and a physical rescue.

8

Red Sea Baptism

Moreover, brethren, I do not want you to be unaware that all our fathers were under the cloud, all passed through the sea, all were baptized into Moses in the cloud and in the sea...
(1 Corinthians 10:1–2)

The Israelites' salvation journey initially involved a fight on the enemy's turf, in which they learned it was the Lord who would fight their battles. In fact, God set up a naturally impossible situation so His supernatural power would be evident. The children of Israel left Egypt with carts laden with gold, silver, and clothes from their Egyptian neighbours (Exodus 12:35–36). I imagine they were thinking, 'Praise God, it's over! Soon we will arrive in our new land.'

In new covenant terms, I liken this stage to the threshold of accepting Jesus as Saviour. We are learning He is good, and He desires a relationship. Although we may not know a lot about Him, we are keen to know more and step into all He offers (especially those treasures). We might assume our troubles are behind us and life will be milk and honey forever after. But no… there is much more to walk through on our spiritual journey. Jesus becomes our guide, and we are His excited new followers.

Will God Come Through?

So the excited new followers of this powerful God of Abraham, Isaac, and Jacob celebrated their way out of Egypt. Their Lord went before them during the day in the form of a pillar of cloud, and he gave them a pillar of fire by night (Exodus 13:21). I love the term pillar as it reminds us our God is central to holding everything else in our lives up! If our little buildings lose their pillar of support, they will collapse. Oh, how we need to remember God is our pillar and place that pillar as a central support structure around which we build our lives.

Suddenly, after only a short time out of Egypt, an incensed Pharaoh chased the Israelites down to force them back into slavery. Have you had the enemy come at you shortly after your decision to follow the Lord out of your chaotic situation? Did troubles arise just before or after you were baptised? I believe the enemy of our Lord absolutely does not want us baptised, but if we are—he wants to lull us into a sleepy spiritual state where we believe it is only a symbolic ritual with no power. I firmly believe our Lord does absolutely nothing that is 'just' symbolic or for a ritualistic measure! He is a God of power, not of performance.

Now there is symbolism *in* baptism. But baptism is much more than symbolic. I truly believe something tangible happens in the spirit realm when we are baptised! Why does Jesus stress the importance of baptism, and why does Peter link baptism with repentance (Acts 2:38)? I don't think we've begun to unlock the power of baptism in most of our church communities.

With the Egyptian army closing in behind them and the Red Sea blocking their path, the Israelites were terrified, and Moses had to reassure them. To this group of newly rescued ex-slaves, the entire journey was one big, uncertain unknown. Would this God who called them out of Egypt with signs and wonders deliver on His promises? Or was it to end on the shores of the Red Sea? The concerned people asked Moses if he had deliberately taken them out of Egypt to die in the wilderness (Exodus 14:11–12). I feel their pain. What a daunting sight and a vulnerable position.

Sure, there's a pillar of cloud with you reminding you of the presence of God—but you haven't experienced Him personally at this point, and your mind is spinning to protect your little ones and your fragile existence. This is a powerful scene of how faith stretches you! Will I believe in the One who called me into His confidence and His kingdom, or will I become overwhelmed at the visible signs of the enemy's encroachment? A tough choice, but each day we are invited to make it as the enemy pursues, taunts, and tries to intimidate us.

Baptism is much more than symbolic.

What happens next is definitely extraordinary, and no special effects crew could capture its magnificence or the emotion and wonder of the scene. A strong wind rises from the east after Moses stretches his hand over the sea. Hidden behind the pillar of fire, the Israelites watch and wait. Two enormous walls of water appear—and the dry ground becomes their path between the glassy walls. I note the word says *dry* land. Surely, it was wet? No, it says the land between the watery walls was dry. No Israelite would get stuck in the boggy bottom of the sea, struggling to manoeuvre their donkeys and carts across.

Dry land came to their aid and hastened their passing. Wow! Imagine this powerful picture for a moment.

Not so for the proud and arrogant Pharaoh and his soldiers. 'Ah-ha!' Pharaoh thinks to himself. 'Gotcha!' Who was he kidding?

> *Now it came to pass, in the morning watch, that the LORD looked down upon the army of the Egyptians through the pillar of fire and cloud, and He troubled the army of the Egyptians. And He took off their chariot wheels, so that they drove them with difficulty; and the Egyptians said, "Let us flee from the face of Israel, for the LORD fights for them against the Egyptians.* (Exodus 14:24–25)

Freedom!

The Almighty had led Pharaoh into a trap (Exodus 14:1–4). It was Pharaoh's choice to continue to harass the children of God, breaking his word again. It was Pharaoh's arrogance and action that led him to his watery grave, along with his entire army. Not a single one was left. This profound act of God was breathtaking and final in terms of His deliverance, and it is one of the most recorded and re-told stories of the Israelites. The message has much value for us today. What can we learn from it?

The Baptism

The children of Israel had obeyed God's commandments for Passover and did everything He told them to prepare for their rescue from Egypt. By faith, they followed Moses into the wilderness lands. Passing through the waters of the Red Sea was a baptism. The cloud (God's presence) and the water (God's deliverance) are named as components of this baptism.

Moreover, brethren, I do not want you to be unaware that all our fathers were under the cloud, all passed through the sea, all were baptized into Moses in the cloud and in the sea...
(1 Corinthians 10:1–2)

Moses was a type of Christ, hence the baptism 'into Moses'. He was the saviour to the children of Israel and mediator of the first covenant. Baptism formed part of the salvation process for the Israelites:

1. Passover—partaking of the lamb, which represented Jesus, the Lamb of God.

2. Exodus—turning their back on the world they once knew to follow their God.

3. Red Sea—baptised into Moses, who represented God's word and His Son until Jesus came and made a new covenant.

The Deliverance

The enemy was completely and utterly wiped out when the sea walls came crashing down. God Himself caused the chariot wheels of the enemy to fall off, ceasing their motion (Exodus 14:25). He washed this powerful, arrogant enemy away in the sea, never to be seen again. (Well, they have more recently found some archaeological evidence of Egyptian chariots on the Red Sea floor, but that is a story for another time!)

We see a principle of baptism in this watery grave. We are called to be buried in Christ and raised to new life in Him through His resurrection:

> *For you were buried with Christ when you were baptized. And with him you were raised to new life because you trusted the mighty power of God, who raised Christ from the dead.* (Colossians 2:12 NLT)

In Colossians 2:15, Paul arrives at one of the most powerful and exciting verses in Scripture! He proclaims Christ won a public victory over a shamed and disarmed enemy. Christ literally took the enemy's weapon away from him. What was this primary weapon? It was the ultimate spiritual separation of God and us—death. The enemy achieved this by inviting Eve and then her husband to sin. Instead, Jesus invites us to partake of His death in which He defeated sin and in His resurrection, which forever defeated death. In the watery grave of baptism, we leave the enemy's works behind.

Do we see the pattern yet? First, the Israelites—God's firstborn—go through a salvation process that includes deliverance in baptism and annihilation of their enemy. Next, the new covenant children of God go through a salvation process in Jesus, which includes deliverance in baptism because Jesus thoroughly defeated our enemy. Baptism is, therefore, a part of the full salvation work of Jesus Christ (saved—healed—delivered).

The Clean Start

The water baptism decisively separated the Israelites from their past and their bondage. Their enemy was destroyed, and a watery grave lay between them and their previous state of existence. This was a clean start, separating them completely from the misery of Egypt. The Red Sea baptism that destroyed the enemy protected the Israelites and delivered them into new life.

For we died and were buried with Christ by baptism. And just as Christ was raised from the dead by the glorious power of the Father, **now we also may live new lives.** (Romans 6:4 NLT, emphasis mine)

The Red Sea crossing is a hard-won battle and a decisive victory. It foretells what Jesus would do at Calvary, completely and utterly defeating the enemy of the grave. It is a picture of how we will also receive our deliverance.

Unlike many of our procedures for baptism today, I do not see any principle of waiting until we are baptised. I see the decision to follow Christ wrapped up in baptism. (Repentance must be present, or it is simply a bath.) We can take our cue from the Ethiopian eunuch. When he heard the good news of the gospel for the first time, he asked Philip as they passed some water, 'What would keep me from being baptised?' Philip responded with, 'If you believe with all your heart, you may'. And so he stopped his chariot immediately, and Philip baptised him (Acts 8:26–40). When your heart gets the revelation, you shouldn't hesitate!

If you are waiting for your clean start and you acknowledge Jesus as Lord, then baptism is your next stop. (A note: some of you reading this may be concerned as you physically cannot bring this about, whether by health or other barriers. Don't worry! Remember God is your Deliverer, and He will make a way. Pray about this—and be at peace, acknowledging Jesus as your Lord.)

Water and the Word

Martin Luther, the renowned Protestant Reformer, clearly believed baptism was far more than just symbolic. He also believed in the powerful connection of water and word, stating: 'Baptism is not simply plain water. Instead, it is water enclosed in God's command and connected with God's Word.'[1] As Luther points out, God has decreed baptism, and the Word and water are connected. Jesus is the Word of God in all fullness, and His Spirit is living water to us (see the Samaritan woman at the well, John 4). Baptism doesn't wash the outside clean. It announces God has cleaned the inside!

Interestingly, while stripping baptism of its Roman Catholic additions, Luther retained 'exorcism' of the devil as part of the baptismal process.[2] In this, he recognised the sin of Adam is inherent in every human, and the enemy of our souls is the responsible party. The enemy enslaves us *until* Christ frees us. It would appear Luther had a deep grasp of baptism and knew it did a deeply spiritual work, including separating us from the enemy of God.

> *Baptism doesn't wash the outside clean. It announces God has cleaned the inside!*

When we are baptised, we acknowledge the death of our old life. As we come out of the water, we make a statement that we are reborn into Christ's victorious new life by faith in His work (Colossians 2:12). The devil sees this and hopes sincerely we do not fully understand the power we now stand in. Baptism shows the devil again and again that Jesus conquered and saved us from death in the process. Do you think he would enjoy watching his defeat again and again? Baptism is both a spiritual work and an overt declaration against him.

The Baptism of Noah

The Lord knows what baptism means for the enemy in your life. If you are not convinced by now, perhaps the story of Noah will help. Noah was also saved through water and by holding onto the word of God. The following is told by Peter (the preacher is Christ):

> *So he went and preached to the spirits in prison—those who disobeyed God long ago when God waited patiently while Noah was building his boat. Only eight people were saved from drowning in that terrible flood. And that water is a picture of baptism, which now saves you, not by removing dirt from your body, but as a response to God from a clean conscience. It is effective because of the resurrection of Jesus Christ.* (1 Peter 3:19–21 NLT)

Noah and his family were saved by being placed in an ark (a special sealed boat). I think the old Wycliffe translation helps us to better understand the connection between Noah's story and baptism. Wycliffe translates that baptism 'makes us *safe*,' just like God made Noah and his family safe in the waters of the Flood. What was the Flood's purpose? God used its destructive force to cleanse the world of the profound evil that had dominated it. Like the Red Sea, God used the Flood to take out a powerful enemy. God kept Noah and his family of seven safe throughout this process.

The word *diasózó* is used in 1 Peter when referring to the souls saved on the ark. It comprises the words *diá* and *sózó*, which together denote a complete or thorough rescue (saving) and literally means 'to save all the way across'.[3] In other words, it was a full deliverance in which God took Noah and his family from extreme danger to complete safety. Noah's story also reveals God's people were saved through a body of water while their enemy was destroyed by it.

I believe this spiritual reality holds true today, and baptism is a much-needed process in our salvation walk. The effectiveness of baptism is the resurrection of Christ.

> *God not only saved us from something;*
> *He saved us to something.*

Christ's resurrection defeated the enemy completely (Colossians 2:15), and He brings us safely and 'all the way across'. The Father seals us into Christ's death (like He sealed Noah in the ark, safe amidst the Flood of death), and He raises us to life in Christ's resurrection (the defeat over death, bringing new life).

When Noah emerged from the ark, safe from harm, God had brought about new life on the previously destroyed planet. Without this new life, Noah and his family would *not* have survived. We need saving from death and destruction, but we also must have a new life! God not only saved us from something; He saved us *to* something. Aren't these patterns of Scripture remarkable? Noah's story tells us God is our life-giver and He plans ahead for us.

The Red Sea grave was a watery one, as was the grave of the Flood. It seems that God, in His wisdom, has designated baptism as a watery grave for sin and death—our enemies.

Follow the Leader

Even Jesus was baptised. He is the firstborn of God in the ultimate sense and therefore goes first, and we follow. But if Jesus was baptised, it couldn't be because sin had separated Him from God. He was sinless. In fact, Jesus was stepping into His ministry as the great High Priest (Hebrews 7–10) to replace Aaron's priestly lineage. Jesus knew He had to be baptised to 'fulfil all righteousness' (Matthew 3:15). What righteousness? He was referring to the righteous fulfilment of *consecration* so Israel's High Priest could minister before God.

Cleansing and ritual immersion are interwoven into Jewish life. God set up cleansing routines for His people, which revealed His requirement for holiness and was a literal expression of cleanness before a holy God. We see the first occasion of this at Mount Sinai before God delivered His commandments (Exodus 19:10). Then Aaron and his sons were consecrated before their priestly ministry could begin. This process involved removing their clothes, washing, and putting on the clean and prescribed garments of the priesthood *before* being anointed for service (Exodus 40).

As the fulfilment of the Mosaic covenant (the covenant God made with the Israelites through Moses), Jesus had to fulfil this righteous requirement to begin His priestly ministry on Earth. Only when He had been consecrated (baptism) could He receive the anointing for ministry. There is also a sense of consecration when we are baptised, publicly declaring our allegiance to our God.

It is a privilege that we become members of the priesthood of believers when we are saved by Christ (1 Peter 2). Like the priests of Israel who ministered before God, God calls us to be ministers of His gospel! We have been cleansed by the washing of the Word (having received the revelation of the Word by the Spirit), and the blood of Jesus declares our righteousness (belief in His salvation work transfers His righteousness to us). It is a powerful and deeply spiritual work. Religion is so bad for us because it presumes we can work our way into God's 'good books'. But this work belongs to Jesus.

When believers are baptised, we are baptised into Christ. The days of Moses are well past, but he was prophet and saviour for a time, just as the bulls, goats, and lambs were a sacrifice for a time. The stories of Noah and Moses reveal baptism preceded the coming of Messiah. God obviously holds baptism in high regard.

In the watery grave of baptism, we leave the enemy's works behind.

9

Questioning God's Provision

When the Spirit took Jesus into the wilderness, Jesus was walking out something BIG. There was intention in the Spirit's leading. Centuries earlier, the Spirit led God's people out of Egypt and into the wilderness. As their Saviour, Jesus had to fulfil aspects of their journey. During the forty days of fasting in the wilderness alone, He walked the spiritual steps of the Israelites as they journeyed with God for forty years. During this forty-year period, the Israelites succumbed to three big temptations. When the devil came to Jesus, offering bread and kingdoms, the essence of the temptations was the same:

1. Doubting God's provision and complaining (being ruled by the stomach)

2. Idolatry

3. Testing God

For each temptation the Israelites faced and failed to avoid, Jesus, in a physically weakened state, having no food for forty days, triumphed over them. He is proof of being the fulfilment of both law and prophets, and no less so than in the intriguing scene where Satan brings temptation on silver platters and Jesus bats each temptation away with the power of God's word. We will cover the first temptation in this chapter. It's a big one. The ease with which we can fall into this temptation provides a warning to us.

Is God Provider?

When we read the story of the Israelites' journey around the wilderness, we see they had a strong tendency to complain about the menu. I have to confess to having some understanding of this. Personally, I don't enjoy eating the same food day after day. I have some regular and staple favourites, but I don't think I'd enjoy them after several months, much less several years. So while I recognise the need to treat God's word and requirements with care, I acknowledge food and drink are important to us humans!

It is sobering to realise Eve's temptation was couched in a luscious piece of fruit, and Esau gave away his birthright for a bowl of stew. Esau was the firstborn twin of Isaac and Rebekah. By birthright, he should have been the grandson of Abraham to begin the nation of Israel. However, he sold his birthright for a bowl of red lentil stew and some bread to mop it up with (Genesis 25). What!?

The stomach is a powerful dictator, so let's not become disdainful when we read the Israelites grumbled and complained about their food options not long into their wilderness journey. In fact, only *three days* after the spectacular Red Sea miracle, the children grumbled at Moses about water (Exodus 15:22–24). God provided a life-giving tree to sweeten the bitter waters at Marah (a picture of Jesus bringing life to our bitter state!). Immediately after this first bout of complaining, God tested the people. He told them:

> *If you will give earnest heed to the voice of the* LORD *your God, and do what is right in His sight, and give ear to His commandments, and keep all His statutes, I will put none of the diseases on you which I have put on the Egyptians; for I, the* LORD, *am your healer.* (Exodus 15:26 NASB95)

First, He showed them He was Deliverer, and then He revealed Himself as Healer by healing the bitter waters. God also established regulations. By listening to their God and obeying Him, they would remain healthy. Twelve springs of water and seventy date palms were then promptly provided as a camping destination. Do you get the picture? How long do you think they waited to make another complaint? It took them from between the plump date palms at Elim until the next wilderness region called Sin. The entire group of the sons of Israel put in a formal complaint about the menu at this point:

> *Oh, that we had died by the hand of the* LORD *in the land of Egypt, when we sat by the pots of meat and when we ate bread to the full! For you have brought us out into this wilderness to kill this whole assembly with hunger.* (Exodus 16:3)

(Try reading that with a Shakespearean theatrical mopping of the brow for effect.)

My summary is this: 'We would have preferred to die as captives under Pharaoh's cruel hand with adequate food supply than to starve out here'. If I was being less gracious, I might add, 'In this God-forsaken wilderness'. God *was* gracious. This is the point where He promises quail and manna from heaven (Exodus 16). There will be meat for the evening meal and bread for breakfast. The heavenly manna seeds could be ground and baked into cakes with the delicious flavour of pastry and oil (Numbers 11:8). On the sixth day, God would provide double the meal, so the people could rest on the seventh day. Surely this plan would be acceptable?

Well, apparently, the regulations for manna collection were not deemed worthy of adherence. The consequence was deteriorating food in their tents that bred worms—how revolting! However, things didn't improve. These gourmet food critics continued their gastronomic complaints.

Majorly annoyed, God promised a large food delivery of quail to last an entire month. They could eat to their heart's content. But… eventually, quail would come out of their nostrils, and they would become disgusted by it (Numbers 11:20). True to His word, God whipped up a wind that served a bountiful, thick carpet of quail several feet high. The people greedily feasted on quail until God's anger was aroused enough to send a 'very great plague' (11:33). Why did God act so strongly? Because the people had *despised* the Lord who rescued them (Numbers 11:20). Despising the Lord and His provision was no small matter.

From the wilderness of Sin to Rephidim, they struck another water issue (so soon?). Moses is getting somewhat exasperated by this stage of the journey. Again, the people make accusations of being taken into the wilderness to die. Poor Moses seriously thinks his time on Earth may have come to an end, as the people become irate. This place is Massah (remember that!), where the people test the Lord and question whether He is with them (Exodus 17:7). God instructs Moses to strike a rock, and it produces water. Crisis averted. Well, sort of—after the death of Aaron, the complaining escalated.

The well-known fiery serpent episode shows how bad this cyclic issue of complaining was, but it also reveals an unusual but powerful picture of God's grace.

Israel had just won a decisive victory against the king of Arad who had taken some Israelites prisoner. They made a vow to God that if He delivered the enemy into their hand, they would destroy Arad's cities (Numbers 21). But the people seemed to be better at war than they were at dining. Sadly, the people's food complaint repeated in startling similarity to the Sin and Massah incidents:

> *And the people spoke against God and against Moses: "Why have you brought us up out of Egypt to die in the wilderness? For there is no food and no water,* **and our soul loathes this worthless bread.** (Numbers 21:5 emphasis mine)

Our soul loathes this worthless bread? No wonder God became angry with them! They refused to trust in His word and provision. Further, they despised the *bread from heaven* (manna), which represented Jesus. Paul refers to this sin as tempting Christ (1 Corinthians 10:9). It is certainly true the Bread of Life was despised and rejected by His own when Jesus came to Earth. What a sad prophetic image from the wilderness.

This time God brought the swift judgement of snakes. I can imagine those nasty little desert vipers. Argh! They must have been vicious, being described as fiery, and bringing death to the camp. The very physical ways in which God taught His people show His nature. He doesn't want us to be ignorant of sin and its consequences.

A Scorned Healer

The people came to Moses in desperation, acknowledging it was their sin that caused the snake attack. God's provision was the interesting bronze serpent on a pole, lifted up so all the people could see it. When those who were bitten looked at the curious sight, they were healed. This prophetic image is one of Jesus as the answer, or antidote, for our sin, but it is only as we look to Him as the Saviour on the cross we are healed and protected from sin's bite (death). He says so Himself:

And as Moses lifted up the serpent in the wilderness, even so must the Son of Man be lifted up, that whoever believes in Him should not perish but have eternal life. For God so loved the world that He gave His only begotten Son, that whoever believes in Him should not perish but have everlasting life. (John 3:14–16)

Despite being scorned by His own and this scorn being the reason for the venomous snakes, the Son of God became their rescue. God used the bite of sin to force the children of Israel to look upon the One they despised in their hour of need. The bitter sting of sin causes people to despair and seek their Redeemer's rescue. We need to feel this sting to know we need saving! We cannot lessen the sting of sin in our lives because that would lessen the sacrifice of Jesus.

God is so persistent! He constantly offers life and healing, always pointing us to His Son because He knows that through Jesus, we have life. It is *not* God's will for any to perish (2 Peter 3:9).

The Bread of Life

Jesus was also tempted in the area of the stomach. This was the same powerful temptation that previously worked on the children of Israel. When the devil suggested Jesus turn stones into bread, the thought of bread on His forty-day empty stomach must have been tempting! However, the Son of God was not about to let a little hunger come between Him and His destiny. More than that, He was absolutely not about to listen to the enemy's word over the word of His Father! He trusted the word of His Father completely and put all His hope into Him.

Jesus responded to Satan with a quote from Deuteronomy. The words quoted were Moses' words to the Israelites. Here they are in context, with Jesus' quote in bold:

> *You shall remember all the way which the* LORD *your God has led you in the wilderness these forty years, that He might humble you, testing you, to know what was in your heart, whether you would keep His commandments or not. He humbled you and let you be hungry, and fed you with manna which you did not know, nor did your fathers know, that He might make you understand that* **man does not live by bread alone, but man lives by everything that proceeds out of the mouth of the** LORD.
> (Deuteronomy 8:2–3 NASB95, emphasis mine)

When Jesus came to Earth to His Jewish family, these descendants of the children of Israel knew the story of God's provision in the wilderness. Jesus revealed Himself to them as Bread from heaven. The first occasion was for a crowd of five thousand. When the disciples were perplexed at how to feed them, Jesus said, 'Bring them here to Me' (Matthew 14:18). Not only was every person fed and full, but there was also plenty left over. He is the God of 'more than enough'. A short time later, He repeated this miracle to four thousand people in a wilderness area to bring the point home (Matthew 15:33).

It privileges us to know Jesus as the Bread of Life. This daily manna provision reminds me the loving-kindness of the Lord is something we can rely on with absolute certainty, and His provision and loving-kindness are new for every morning of our lives (Lamentations 3:21–23).

A Lesson from Abraham

One of the biggest issues for the Israelites was to learn to trust God as Provider. Abraham shows us what trusting in the Lord's provision really looks like. Genesis 22 is a difficult chapter, but we need to understand it. In the opening verse, God acknowledges He is *testing*

Abraham. This is not a simple test of trusting God for your dinner. This is an extremely difficult test and one I believe most of us would fail outright before it had begun. After waiting until Abraham was an elderly man to give him a promised son, God asked him to sacrifice this son to Him as a burnt offering. Note Abraham's response:

> *So Abraham rose early in the morning and saddled his donkey....* (Genesis 22:3).

Abraham didn't even argue or question God! He just saddled his donkey, packed up his son and some wood, and 'came to the place of which God had told him' (22:9). Remember, this is a test. God did not mean for Abraham to kill his son. He cannot break His own laws. God was testing to see if Abraham would be obedient to whatever He would ask of him because the destiny of nations was resting on him. When Isaac asked his dad where the lamb was for the burnt offering they were going to make, Abraham told him God would provide a lamb for His offering (Genesis 22:7–8).

Abraham passed this test with such flying colours that we know him millennia later for his incredible faith! When the Lord urgently prevented him from sacrificing his boy, sending a ram instead, Abraham named the place of the encounter 'The-Lord-Will-Provide' (22:14).[1] When we sing about Yahweh Yireh (Jehovah Jireh), do we know what this cost the man who coined the name?

It became profoundly apparent to me as I was writing this that Abraham's descendants were definitely not living out the faith of their father. Before we judge these unbelieving wilderness wanderers, we should first ask ourselves:

- Do I believe the stories of God's miraculous power handed down to me in the Bible?

- Do I believe enough to put my faith in God as Provider when my situation says otherwise?

Abraham's faith is the faith we should aspire to. I wonder if, most of the time, we compare more accurately with the wandering Israelites!

The loving-kindness of the Lord is something we can rely on with absolute certainty, and His provision and loving-kindness are new for every morning of our lives.

10

Testing and Mocking God

Nor should we put Christ to the test, as some of them did, and then died from snakebites. And don't grumble as some of them did, and then were destroyed by the angel of death. These things happened to them as examples for us. They were written down to warn us who live at the end of the age. (1 Corinthians 10:9–11 NLT)

Years of sitting in church pews gave me a narrow perspective, and in the days of wooden benches, enough discomfort to keep me awake! Law numbed me from exploring relationship with this God I was called to fear. I was a child in the days of the fire and brimstone preachers, and it was a relief to exit my pew at the conclusion of such sermons. As I have since learned—Mount Sinai is a burden.

When you don't know who God is, you will make a god up. The Israelites were not the only experts at this! Our trust in God cannot grow from a tainted imagination. Is your god distant, angry or more akin to a genie in a bottle? While God is extremely patient, we need to heed the warning about what happens when we test Him.

Testing, Testing, One, Two

The second temptation of Christ involved the devil taking Jesus to the temple's pinnacle and enticing Him to throw Himself off. This outrageous attempt was designed to get Jesus to put God's Word to the test and was based on a prophecy about Jesus in Psalm 91. The Psalm refers to the one who dwells in the shelter of the Most High (91:1), who angels will guard and lift up, preventing them from striking their foot against a stone (91:12). Jesus is quick to respond with Scripture, 'You must not test the Lord your God', which is a partial quote from Deuteronomy:

You must not test the L*ORD* *your God as you did when you complained at* **Massah***.* (6:16 NLT, emphasis mine)

Now, Massah is where Moses produced water from the rock after the people became confrontational about not having water. This is where they tested the Lord, asking if He was with them or not (Exodus 17:7). The temptation was to get God to prove Himself, to push Him to show He is God. God doesn't pander to people who egg Him to perform His 'God duties'. Satan was outrageous in his attempt! He wanted to see if Jesus would try His Father at His word and get God to prove Himself. Jesus handled the devil promptly and succinctly with the Word of God, once again defeating him. However, testing God was an ongoing issue for the Israelites.

Psalm 78 provides a brilliant summary of the story of Israel and how they continually tested God. It's definitely worth a read! Here's an excerpt to give you a taste:

But they sinned even more against Him
By rebelling against the Most High in the wilderness.
And they tested God in their heart

By asking for the food of their fancy.
Yes, they spoke against God:
They said, "Can God prepare a table in the wilderness?
Behold, He struck the rock,
So that the waters gushed out,
And the streams overflowed.
Can He give bread also?
Can He provide meat for His people?
(Psalm 78:17–20)

A Covenant People

By the third month of wilderness travel, the Lord determines to provide these grumbling food critics with His requirements. It is still early days, and God graciously acknowledges His people are still getting to know Him. He doesn't punish them for their grumblings. However, the grace period is coming to a close.

God orchestrates an encounter at Mount Sinai, where He first provides the Israelites with the Ten Commandments in verbal form (Exodus 19–20). Before this encounter, He instructed Moses to prepare the people to be attended by a holy God. They washed their clothes as a sign of cleansing, and Moses consecrated them. The Lord determined this mountain to be holy. Under no circumstances were the people or their animals to touch it. First, God established the boundaries and conditions He required to meet with Him. Next, the masterly Teacher commands their attention with a grand display!

A smoking mountain, complete with thunder, lightning, trembling, a thick cloud, and a loud trumpet, would have been sensory overload! Of course, God had their attention. He gives the Ten Commandments beginning with 'I am the Lord your God' (Exodus 20). This is the first time God addresses His people directly. Their response is to freak out and beg Moses to be God's mouthpiece instead because they fear for their lives. Moses wisely responds with:

> *"Don't be afraid,"* Moses answered them, *"for God has come in this way to test you, and so that your fear of him will keep you from sinning!"* (Exodus 20:20 NLT)

But the people stood at a distance, and only Moses approached God.

> *We cannot develop a relationship with God through our leaders.*

Are there times when we would prefer to hear from a leader rather than the Holy Spirit? We may distance ourselves from Him for a variety of reasons, including fear, ritual, or a deep conviction of His holiness, birthing an awareness of our sinful state. But we cannot develop a relationship with God through our leaders. Moses developed a relationship with God because he was willing to approach Him. Throughout his journey with Israel, he spent time with God to get to know Him personally. Sometimes I think we like to 'get to know' God through the safety of the guy in the pulpit. But as the children of Israel proved, that is a self-defeating position.

At this point in our story, God provides Moses with the detail of His covenant. The terms outlined how to remain in relationship with Him. He included social, legal, property, justice, moral, ceremonial, and feast requirements, amongst others. Moses carefully relayed all these requirements to the people, and they dutifully responded, promising to keep all of God's laws (Exodus 24:3). Remember, this is a covenant in the making!

The next morning, Moses builds an altar and makes burnt offerings and peace offerings before the Lord at the foot of the mountain. He reads all God's words to the people, words he has now carefully scribed. I imagine he stayed up all night to do this! Again, the people agree to follow *all* God's laws. So Moses takes blood from the sacrifices and sprinkles the people (Exodus 24:8). This is their consecration according to the covenant they have just agreed to. For the second time since God called Moses to lead them from captivity, they find themselves under the blood of a covenant.

I've taken the time to outline the scene before we get to one of the biggest head-scratching moments of Israel's journey to Promise. While I can understand grumbling tummies, I find it incredibly difficult to understand what happened to their resolve to adhere to God's covenants. Now they have a set of agreed rules, with a blood covenant no less! But God hasn't quite finished with Moses. There is more to impart. So, Moses heads up the mountain for an extended period with Him to take down requirements for the Tabernacle, the priesthood, the sacrifices, and all associated details of how to worship and approach the holy God of Israel. Moses leaves Aaron in charge at the bottom of the mountain. Oh, Aaron. What were you thinking?

No Idolatry Here!

Even after the powerful and awe-inspiring display of God at the mountain, the people were quick to give up on Moses and God's instructions about not making any image of a god or worshipping it. When they approached Aaron to request he make them a god to lead them, Aaron didn't even appear to hesitate. In fact, you might think he had experience in this area. Quickly, the people tore off their gold earrings and brought them to Aaron.

Aaron must have had some craftsman skill because he took a tool and fashioned a calf from the melted gold. Next, he built an altar before the calf and proclaimed a feast for the Lord for the following day, effectively mixing the worship of God Most High with a false god. Maybe he was trying to redeem the awful thing he had done. I don't know. But the next day, they made burnt offerings along with peace offerings, and they hosted a less than savoury event.

We are told the people rose up to 'play', which may sound like modern-day partying, but the root word has connotations of mocking and making sport of something.[1] Were they mocking the God of Israel? It would appear so. After all, in reference to the calf, they said, 'This is your god, O Israel, who brought you up from the land of Egypt' (Exodus 32:4). As God watched on, He relayed this scene to Moses on the mountain. I can only imagine the look on poor Moses' face when he heard these words. The God who had just delivered them from Pharaoh with mighty wonders was mocked and quickly replaced by a mute idol created by human hands. Not just any human hands, either. It was the hands of the soon-to-be High Priest of Israel!

Worshipping another god was one thing. It would appear likely the people had been doing this in Egypt by how quickly they formed a god-manufacturing group. However, mocking the God of Israel was quite another. Without Moses' intercession, the Lord may well have destroyed them right there. God was ready to begin the process of building His nation again with Moses (Exodus 32:10).

Moses was furious. He administered immediate punishment by making the children of Israel drink the ground-up golden calf, forcing them to partake of their god! He chastised his brother, who feigned ignorance, and called together a group who was still loyal to God. When the sons of Levi stepped forward, Moses gave them the confronting task of meting out punishment with their swords. God also punished the people with a plague. He could do nothing else. He had made a covenant of blood.

When recapping this story to the Israelites at the end of their forty-year journey, Moses says, 'I took the two tablets and threw them out of my two hands and broke them before your eyes' (Deuteronomy 9:17). His action appears to be deliberate—not accidental or rage-induced. We see a prophetic act in line with the peoples' actions in the natural—the breaking of commandments. Moses actively mourned and fasted, grieved by their sins, and fearful God would destroy them. God *would* have destroyed Aaron had it not been for Moses' prayers.

It is so sad to see the pattern of Israel's idolatry. They were quick to forget the golden calf incident and God's commandments. Some men went after the Moabite women at Acacia Grove, also joining in with the worship of their god (Numbers 25). We see a strong connection between idolatry and sexual immorality through the Israelites' story. One led to the other. This issue not only plagued the wilderness generation, but it was also a heart matter that resulted in Babylonian captivity and the grief and wailing of many of God's prophets. It was difficult for the Israelites to separate from the ways of Egypt.

The Process of Yielding

Jesus met the tempter on the temptation of idolatry too, and also at a mountain location. There is something about high places (mountains) and worship. Of course, Satan is the master counterfeiter who envied the high places of God when he was still a God-worshipping chief cherub (Ezekiel 28). He has not lost his desire for the high places of worship. It is no wonder that in his terrestrial rule, he commandeers mountains and demands people to worship him on them. In return, he offers a little something. Beware—he never trades fairly!

In the last temptation, Satan tried to trade with Jesus, offering Him world kingdoms if He would bow down and worship him (seriously?). Without hesitation, Jesus told the enemy to leave Him alone, adding,

'You shall worship the LORD your God, and serve Him only' (Matthew 4:10 NASB), which Jesus quoted from God's word to Moses and the Israelites. We arrive at the result of three for three temptations in Jesus' favour. Defeated, Satan had to leave, proving the words of James that if we:

- Submit to God (including His word); and

- Resist the devil (with God's word); then

- The devil will have to flee from us (because his lies are defeated with God's truth).

The key is in the submission (James 4:7). Note how Jesus defeated Satan with the word of God, *and* He took authority and told him to leave. Satan had to obey, determining to wait until another opportunity presented (Luke 4:13).

The difference between the Israelites' wilderness journey and the temptation of Jesus is in the submission—His obedience to the word of God.

Several years ago, the Lord helped me come to terms with the word *submit*. I did not like this word! To me, the word held connotations of being forced into an inferior or secondary position. The way God helped me understand the meaning was to use a related word. He impressed upon me the word *yield*. I was not in the habit of using the word yield. In fact, I headed to the dictionary and a thesaurus for some deeper insight.

Yielding helped explain the process of release—of letting go and voluntarily placing my will under the will of God. Yield, as a verb, has surrender as part of its meaning.[2] It also has the definition of harvest and return on an investment when a crop or a financial investment produces. The yielding process is one of surrender—surrendering our ideas, opinions, and pride to take up God's concrete purpose and hope for our life. To me, the word submit had cracked down like a religious whip, decreeing my head bow and my knees fold. Not so because our God created us for relationship, which by nature is a two-way process involving a willing association and attachment.

> *The difference between the Israelites' wilderness journey and the temptation of Jesus is in the submission—His obedience to the word of God.*

You cannot have a relationship without willingness. God created us with a will, and He desires for us to use our will freely to choose Him and keep choosing Him over the enemy's taunts and temptations. I am so grateful for this lesson! When I know God cares for me so much He gives me the right to choose my submission (my yielded-ness), I am far more likely to lay my will down. There is something about being forced that causes a fiery flame to rise in us! When we are invited, however, we surrender our will more peacefully.

Keep in mind that while the yielding process is on our terms, the outcome of refusing to yield will ultimately bring destruction. Spoiler alert! Sadly, this is the outcome of the Israelite's story. The generation of Israelites that complained, tested God, and were prone to idolatry, did not make it to their land of Promise. That is profoundly heartbreaking. Jesus, on the other hand, went from His temptation straight into ministry. He was found complete in character and obedience. His yielded-ness produced life for us.

The Israelites mocked and tested God because they had not yet come into relationship with Him. They also didn't trust Him. The enemy quickly stole the seeds of the word God gave on Mount Sinai; seeds yet to take root (Parable of the Sower, Matthew 13). A lack of trust and yielded-ness meant the Israelites who exited Egypt, never entered the land of Promise. This is an incredibly important point to understand! Religion cannot take you into your destiny.

I believe yielded-ness comes ultimately from a relationship of trust between God and us. To trust Him, we must get to know Him! Knowing *about* Him is not sufficient. We see this with the mountaintop experience of Moses versus the lower plain experience of the children of Israel. While Moses was resting in the rare mountain air, soaking in the presence of God, the people of Israel turned their thoughts to their immediate circumstances and doubted all they had seen and heard. When we believe spiritual head knowledge and verbal assent to God's word are adequate, we live only in the heavy air of religion.

> *The generation of Israelites that complained, tested God, and were prone to idolatry, did not make it to their land of Promise.*

We come alive when we climb into higher spiritual realms, where God beckons us to join Him. In these places, we are vulnerable. We must rely on God to sustain us, just as God sustained Moses despite eating no food while in his presence. But it is only in the rare mountaintop air we enter relationship. From that place, we learn to trust enough to yield to God's plans and purposes for us. We place ourselves in God's secure hands, knowing He will carry out everything He says He will. Faith removes all doubt. It is the place Jesus remained in while He was on Earth. He stayed in a constant and close relationship with the Father. He trusted Him even to the point of walking out death on a gruesome cross. Without His yielded-ness to the Father, there would be no good news story!

11

Bones in the Wilderness

Many years ago, I read a book titled *The Windshield Is Bigger than the Rear-view Mirror*. Its focus was on getting stuck in the past, and the title has since stuck with me. There is a reason the windshield is bigger. We need to see clearly where we are going. In reality, how often do we get stuck in the past, staring behind us and reminiscing instead of facing the day and the situation we live in? Sometimes we develop nostalgia and gloss over our past issues because what we are facing is uncomfortable, uncertain, or even painful. Maybe we fear our future. Maybe the windshield (or windscreen where I come from) appears too big, and we can't take in the complete scene before us. But continuing the analogy, it is difficult to drive well or safely if we continue to glance back in our little rear-view mirror.

The Risk of Looking Back

God knows our past can be a trap for us. There was a reason Lot and his family were told not to look back as God brought destruction to their home city of Sodom. Looking back cost Lot's wife her life. Can it really be that serious? Well, it would appear this was part of the problem with the children of Israel in the wilderness. They continually looked back, reinterpreting their past and even longing for it and dishonouring the God who had saved them.

We can be in danger of looking back and reinterpreting our past, just like the Israelites did.

Because of where they fixed their eyes, they couldn't see today's blessings. The consequences of their limited view were the same as for Lot's wife. Their bones remained behind in the wilderness while their children and grandchildren proceeded to inherit their Promise. I believe God wanted to take families across the Jordan into the land of Promise. Passover revealed He was the God who visited households and protected households from harm. He is a God of family and He doesn't want to see anyone left behind.

Whatever the reason, we can be in danger of looking back and reinterpreting our past, just like the Israelites did. Somehow, they reinterpreted the painful and subjected position they were in during their time in Egypt, and no doubt exercised some selective memory. Were the meat pots really that good? Did the bread on the table at night really make up for living under subjugation and at Pharaoh's mercy? Did they remember an entire generation of men was almost lost because of the jealousy and brutality of this Egyptian king? It would appear not. Their stomachs caused them to review the story with a rose-tinted lens and a thick helping of gravy.

> *Oh, that we had died by the hand of the* LORD *in the land of Egypt, when we sat by the pots of meat and when we ate bread to the full!* (Exodus 16:3)

If I remember the story correctly, it was not the hand of the Lord against them in Egypt! It was His hand that delivered them *from* Egypt. In fact, Scripture refers to His strong and mighty hand. It would appear their stomachs are talking at this point.

As we have seen with Israel, there may be times in our lives when the temptation to go back is strong. The Lord's hand may seem slow or distant, or the enemy's lies may be loud and proud as he tries to convince you to turn back.

> *For it would have been better for us to serve the Egyptians than that we should die in the wilderness.* (Exodus 14:12)

The writer of Hebrews wrote the following warning through the Holy Spirit. This is one of those 'you'd better listen up' moments:

> *Today when you hear his voice, don't harden your hearts as Israel did when they rebelled, when they tested me in the wilderness. There your ancestors tested and tried my patience, even though they saw my miracles for forty years. So I was angry with them, and I said, "Their hearts always turn away from me. They refuse to do what I tell them." So in my anger I took an oath: "They will never enter my place of rest."* (Hebrews 3:7–11 NLT)

They are very challenging words.

A Stiff-necked People

The Hebrews' writer continues with, 'You must warn each other every day, while it is still "today" so that none of you will be deceived by sin and hardened against God' (3:13 NLT). It must be a very important point for us to get because the writer repeats it two verses later, 'Today when you hear his voice, don't harden your hearts as Israel did when they rebelled'. I read a plea, an exhortation here. The author, under the inspiration of God's Spirit, has emphasised this point. We need to listen—we need to listen *today*.

We must keep our hearts from becoming hard. Rebellion is an act of pride against God, and it is caused by a hardening of the heart. This was the issue of Pharaoh, who refused to let God's people go. It is wilful and deliberate. It tries God by questioning Him, and when He doesn't come up with the desired answers, the person places themselves into His position in their life and follows the desires of their hard heart. A hard heart is a spiritually scary matter! Like Pharaoh, there may come a time when the ability to repent is lost.

The Bible is clear about the outcome of rebellion. For Israel, it ended with bodies in the wilderness. These bodies were precious, having been rescued for purpose and Promise. They were somebody's loved one. Most of all, the God who came seeking them for His own loved them. His people rejected Him, and by doing so, they rejected His Promise and lost their purpose. Destiny without God is no destiny. This chapter in Hebrews soberly ends with, 'So we see that because of their unbelief they were not able to enter his rest' (3:19 NLT). The thought of not entering God's rest, whether in this life or the next, should give grave cause for concern and a holy fear.

Rebellion kept the people from Promise, and it's a sin of pride and control—control of one's destiny and an attempt to control God. The Bible tells us rebellion is linked to witchcraft. Witchcraft is not just about spells and potions…

For rebellion is as the sin of witchcraft, and stubbornness is as iniquity and idolatry. (1 Samuel 15:23)

This verse is Samuel speaking to Saul. Notice the repeated use of the words 'is as'. There is more than an analogy here. Rebellion and stubbornness both turn our hearts from God because they focus on us and our human hearts' desires. Idolatry results from stubbornness. This is a spiritual truth! The children of Israel show how this plays out in practice. Their stubborn nature always led them to idolatry. Why? Instead of placing God in prime position on the altar of their hearts, they placed their desires instead. Eventually, idolatry of the heart will manifest openly.

A hard heart is a spiritually scary matter!

But what about rebellion and witchcraft? At Marah, the children of Israel complained about the bitter waters. Marah can mean bitter, but it also means rebellious![1] Marah, in the wilderness, declared physically and spiritually that Jacob's children were rebellious. Ouch. They openly defied the word of the Lord about their inheritance and His provision. Both rebellion and stubbornness result in people rejecting the word of the Lord.

Samuel confirms this truth in his stern rebuke to Saul, 'Because you have rejected the word of the LORD, He also has rejected you from being king' (1 Samuel 15:23). We suddenly see the gravity of rebellion. When we rebel, we tell God His word is not our truth. But somebody's word has to be our truth. Rebellion is to choose a different word.

Saul had developed a habit of kicking God's word to the curb and trying to manipulate Him (1 Samuel 13 and 15). Eventually, Saul reveals the nature of his heart when he visits a clairvoyant, seeking a 'divine' word from the dead Samuel (1 Samuel 28). Divination is a counterfeit of true prophecy and a form of witchcraft. Like the stubborn behaviours that led to idolatry in the wilderness, Saul's rebellious behaviours eventually led to overt sorcery.

Recently, I was listening to a Derek Prince recording,[2] and I was struck by his reference to witchcraft as a work of the *flesh*, not a work of the supernatural. I had to look it up. Sure enough, witchcraft is listed alongside idolatry as a work of the flesh in Galatians 5:20. Perhaps the most colourful and obvious example of witchcraft in Scripture is Queen Jezebel, wife of Ahab. We know her for her manipulation, intimidation, and control over the free will of others. These are seeds of witchcraft.[3] Beware the sin of rebellion! It declares, 'I will do it my way', and witchcraft's false power isn't far behind. (I'd highly recommend Derek's teaching on this important topic.)

> *The encouraging truth about a covenant initiated by God is there is zero chance of Him reneging on any of His vows.*

We are familiar with contracts containing legally binding terms and conditions today. Why do we take God's covenant as being any less? Why are we shocked when He takes action? Like a marriage covenant, when one party doesn't keep their covenant vows, the other party has the right to take action, including dissolving the marriage.

The conditions of God's covenant invite us, like a loved one in a marriage, to partner with Him and receive the blessings of a relationship. He is a God of love and covenant, not control and rules. God won't force a partnership with us, but there are consequences for turning our backs on Him.

The encouraging truth about a covenant initiated by God is there is zero chance of Him reneging on any of His vows. He won't leave us—but like any partnership, we have the *choice* to leave Him. We are then out in the cold unless we humbly return to His forgiveness and relationship. Rebellion says, 'I don't care about You or Your covenant'! Pray for a soft heart towards God to avoid the pride and pain of rebellion.

The people of Israel were 'stiff-necked', according to the Lord. The image of a stiff neck is a picture of an inability to bow, to yield to God's sovereign power and better judgement. This is not a chiropractic issue! Stiff-necked people are rebellious and stubborn with a pride problem. (I can't help but briefly wonder if living in the pride of Egypt for so long rubbed off.) Who is the father of pride? Well, he traces back further than the pharaohs, and Jesus saw him fall from heaven like lightning. Pride always comes before a fall. This is a spiritual principle set in stone we would do well to remember.

It's All Your Fault, God

We would never blame God for our problems, right? Of course, that is not true. Blaming God for our problems is not new. The children of Israel cried out to the Lord with their complaints against Him. It was after one such complaint God came through with His manna and quail. He was gracious to His new group of followers because they were still learning, but also because He loves to provide for His children. But we have seen how testing God does not end well. Testing His patience is not a recommended strategy. There is a point of ignorance I believe God will overlook, such as He did before giving the Israelites their clear set of living instructions. After that, He held them accountable. I am grateful God is merciful to us in our ignorance. However, He also says *His people* die because they lack the knowledge of His ways (Hosea 4:6). Could this apply to us too?

We may allow a small child to beat her fists and scream, arching her back and refusing to cooperate. When we mature, this is no longer considered acceptable! Are we still having tantrums when God doesn't deliver our answers on our terms in our time frames? When we didn't get the express angelic delivery envelope the morning after we said our prayers, do we harden just a bit of our heart? When we pray and pray, and we don't get the answer we hoped for, do we grow a little cold towards Him in our prayers? Is our prayer closet gathering dust? Do we have a little piece of veil over a piece of our heart because we recall a time He didn't come through for us (or so we have believed)? Then the veil becomes a shrine. Maybe there is grief and hurt under that veil. But the veil has become a hidden place no longer touched by the light of His word because at that moment, when it mattered to us—*He* didn't do the thing our heart desired.

In that place, under the veil, lives unbelief. We are good at telling ourselves fairy stories when it suits us. We can create a story that helps (or so we think) with our pain and disappointment. Blaming God is not that difficult, actually. It's amazing how many atheists shake their fists at God during times of disaster and distress. They didn't believe Him beforehand. They are quick to blame Him afterwards. Are we so different?

I end this chapter by posing a challenge. In what areas of your life are you blaming God? Will you stop and talk to Him about it? It's time to remove that piece of veil and protect your heart from getting cold. Raise those hands in prayer, not anger. Confess your unbelief. Ask Him to remove the veil and heal you. It is His delight to bring healing to His children.

12

Fire and Sacrifice

Therefore, since we are receiving a kingdom which cannot be shaken, let us have grace, by which we may serve God acceptably with reverence and godly fear. For our God is a consuming fire. (Hebrews 12:28–29)

The story of Nadab and Abihu should cause us to sit up and take notice. Aaron's sons had just been ordained as priests, and the first offerings were made to God in the new Tabernacle. This was a big event. At the conclusion of this elaborate ceremony, God provided for a dramatic display of fire which consumed the burnt offering (Leviticus 9). The people were overjoyed at His acceptance of their offering. The special ministry of the priests began in accordance with all God's carefully prescribed requirements for ministering before Him. Shortly after this weighty ceremony, for unknown reasons, Nadab and Abihu ignored God's requirements for the ministry of incense. They perverted the ministry of Jesus as represented in the incense offering. Instead, they offered their own form of incense offering and consequently lost their lives by the consuming fire of God (Leviticus 10:2).

This kind of story is confronting, and we may exclaim indignantly that God doesn't do this anymore. But God's views on holy fire have never changed, despite the privilege of living in the new covenant age of grace.

Healing Fire

God's fire both consumes and heals. There is a regulation in Leviticus on how to manage the appearance and spread of mildew (13:47–59). Today, we know how outbreaks of mould and mildew around our homes can be quite serious, even causing long-term health issues for people exposed to the spores. Who knew the Bible had an answer? The process for dealing with mildew outbreaks involved its inspection by the priest. Items were inspected, quarantined, and re-inspected. The mildew was cut out of fabric or other soft materials—or burned if it persisted in spreading.

As believers, we need not fear the holy and consuming fire of God that purifies us from our sin.

Mildew is like sin. If it isn't cut out of the part of our heart it lives in, it will continue to spread through our lives and our relationship with God and others. We need to have regular heart inspections, allowing the Holy Spirit to find any spiritual mildew. Sometimes a quarantine period follows, where we keep ourselves away from temptations, and we work on our hearts in the secret place with God alone. But there is another part to the process. There needs to be purification to eradicate the remaining spores of sin, burning them up by the fire of God.

As believers, we need not fear the holy and consuming fire of God that purifies us from our sin. Like David, we can ask the Holy Spirit to search our hearts and see if there is any spiritual mildew stuck to our hearts in a dark corner somewhere. David is a noble example for us. He sinned, and his sin was a huge breach of God's commandments. David had an affair and deliberately orchestrated the death of Bathsheba's husband to cover up the resulting pregnancy. But in time, he acknowledged his error and, in humility, came to God for His healing.

Religion makes us run from God in times of sin. A relationship causes us to run to God, trusting He always desires reconciliation and a relationship with us. David knew he could place himself in the merciful hands of God. He did not resist the purifying process because he trusted Him.

When Sacrifice Doesn't Work

The sacrifices of Israel were for unintentional sin (Numbers 15). There was no sacrifice for wilful and brazen sin—only punishment, which was the case for Nadab and Abihu. (Praise God for Jesus, right!?) Once you step into covenant with God as the people of Israel did at Mount Sinai, you sign on for the requirements of that covenant. God's feelings around this haven't changed. If we ignore Him and are wilfully rebellious in our behaviour, we open ourselves up for essentially the same punishment—being cut off from our people (ouch).

I encourage you to read the following old and new covenant examples carefully. It may be easy to dismiss Old Testament Scripture that we perceive as harsh or too law based. But I want you to see the principle carry through to the New Testament. And to look further to see God's reasons. He does not act randomly or without reason.

God instructed Moses:

> *But those who brazenly violate the LORD's will, whether native-born Israelites or foreigners, have blasphemed the LORD, and* ***they must be cut off from the community.*** *Since they have treated the LORD's word with contempt and deliberately disobeyed his command, they must be completely cut off and suffer the punishment for their guilt.* (Numbers 15:30–31 NLT, emphasis mine)

Compare that with Paul instructing the Corinthians:

> *When I wrote to you before, I told you not to associate with people who indulge in sexual sin. But I wasn't talking about unbelievers who indulge in sexual sin, or are greedy, or cheat people, or worship idols. You would have to leave the world to avoid people like that. I meant that you are not to associate with anyone* ***who claims to be a believer*** *yet indulges in sexual sin, or is greedy, or worships idols, or is abusive, or is a drunkard, or cheats people.* ***Don't even eat with such people.*** (1 Corinthians 5:9–11 NLT, emphasis mine)

Note carefully that both situations refer to your *spiritual brother*. Paul clarifies we judge each other in the house of God—not those outside of it. Outside is God's domain. But hang on, Paul. Aren't we supposed to just keep loving them back into fellowship? We need some context for these challenging words.

First, a misinterpretation of 'excommunication' has led many believers to live in shame and pain on the outside of the community. The church needs to be a safe place to confess our transgressions and live out our sanctification process. We should expect grace in times of need. Elsewhere, Paul writes about restoring the transgressing believer into fellowship with a spirit of gentleness (Galatians 6:1). James also tells us to confess our sins to each other and pray for each other to enable our healing (5:16). But there is a huge difference between the general principle of forgiveness and keeping each other accountable to live a holy life and pride leading to wilful and deliberate sin (the earlier Corinthians example).

Paul is *not* talking about a repentant person! He is talking about someone who continues to sin wilfully *while* professing to be a believer in Jesus. In this case, it was a churchgoer sleeping with his stepmother. Even the pagans would have blushed. Before Paul pens these stern instructions to the Corinthian church, he speaks in Jewish terms about the spread of leaven through the whole lump of dough. Israel's sin always spread through the camp. This is why Paul urged the fledgling church to remove the cause. Good government acts in the best interests of the *entire* community.

Grace begins and ends with how we treat the Son of God.

To the humble person, we offer grace, and to the conceited person, we offer law (see Proverbs 3:34, James 4:6 and 1 Peter 5:5). Remember, the law is designed to expose our sin and prick our conscience, so in this context, it's a merciful act. In fact, Paul explains to the Corinthians why you let the unrepentant person go. It's an act of chastening them now to *save* them for eternity (1 Corinthians 5:5). Therefore, it's a loving act with a long-term view of God's judgement against sin. Paul knew God wants everyone saved!

The penalty for serious, wilful sin under the Mosaic covenant was severe, even up to death. Our wilful sin and an unrepentant heart result in serious consequences because it is not the sacrifice of bulls and goats we disdain but the sacrifice of Jesus Christ.

When we continue with deliberate sin in disregard of Christ's sacrifice, there is no further sacrifice available (Hebrews 10:26). That should give us cause for sober reflection. God poured His grace out in Jesus. But if we disdain Jesus, there is no further grace. To put it another way, there is no alternate avenue for grace. Grace begins and ends with how we treat the Son of God:

For if we sin wilfully after we have received the knowledge of the truth, there no longer remains a sacrifice for sins, but a certain fearful expectation of judgment, and fiery indignation which will devour the adversaries. (Hebrews 10:26–27)

Anyone who has rejected Moses' law dies without mercy on the testimony of two or three witnesses. Of how much worse punishment, do you suppose, will he be thought worthy who has trampled the Son of God underfoot, counted the blood of the covenant by which he was sanctified a common thing, and insulted the Spirit of grace? For we know Him who said, "Vengeance is Mine, I will repay," says the Lord. And again, "The LORD will judge His people." It is a fearful thing to fall into the hands of the living God. (Hebrews 10:28–31)

If this is you right now, come back into the Father's embrace! He is waiting for *you*, His precious child, to return to Him in humility. Don't let pride stand in your way. Remember, it is not God's will for anyone to be separated from Him! He has gone to great lengths to save you and me. Jesus is our complete answer. And our sin is *erased* by the Father when we accept this truth.

Fire and Oil

John declares Jesus will come and baptise in the Holy Spirit and with fire (Matthew 3). The concept of refining fire appears in multiple passages, referring to the refining process God puts His people 1through. Isaiah 48 and Psalm 66 contain references to the refining of silver. By going through the refining fire, silver has its impurities removed. Therefore, the refining fire of the Spirit is good for us! It may not always feel comfortable at the time, but if we love God and are called to His purposes, He works all these situations out for our good (Romans 8:28). Refining by the Spirit's fire is critical for our sanctification. As we learned in our mildew example, fire is the heavy-duty cleansing process for less than superficial issues.

Beware the tempter who tries to derail you from the tracks of your purpose with strange fire and promises.

Along with requiring refined vessels, God must anoint everything used for His ministry. The anointing oil of the Tabernacle was not for general use, nor was it to be replicated outside the temple environment. In fact, anyone who replicated it, or put it on an outsider, would be cut off from the Lord's people. There have been many occasions through Christendom, and sadly today, when a human-made institution has deemed people suitable for God's holy work, but they are not walking in His ways. God cannot anoint anything unholy! The work is, therefore, a counterfeit with no fruit. Worse, it can damage new believers and prevent their faith's progress.

People can confuse God's love with His anointing and blessing. God is love, but He cannot anoint, bless, or overlook unholy acts. Whether strange fire, like Nadab and Abihu's false offering, unholy alliances and immoral living, jealousy, pride, hatred, or unforgiveness, God will not bless or endorse the professing believer who engages in these things. It doesn't matter if they are the world's most gifted preacher. When God removes the anointing (He selects and anoints His own priesthood), then the gifted person is just—a gifted person. Sadly, we live in a time where many believers have fallen prey to the enemy's deceptions and have lost their anointing for ministry. Their once fruitful ministry dries up, which is exactly what the devil planned for. Beware the tempter who tries to derail you from the tracks of your purpose with strange fire and promises.

The old covenant holds a blueprint for ministry. Moses anointed Aaron and his sons with the oil that represented God's blessing on their ministry. As a member of the priesthood of believers, we are blessed with the anointing of the Spirit of God (1 John 2:27). The Spirit also gives anointed gifts to the body of believers (1 Corinthians 12), much like God gave specific duties to specific artisans and tribes within Israel. It is so easy for us to mix up our natural gifts and desires with the sanctified work of the Spirit. I may decide to move to a faraway country and dedicate myself to ministry, but if that is not His plan for my life, the work may be good, but it is not anointed.

Churches can be very casual with ministry today, forgetting it is God's ministry, not ours. God would not have accepted Moses telling a non-Levite he could minister in the Tabernacle simply because Moses saw a 'servant-heart' or some 'potential.' Why do we put the wrong people—even those who don't know or acknowledge Jesus—in the worship team? They are not there to feel good about themselves! There is also a process for training, equipping, and releasing. Raising and anointing someone for ministry out of their season or calling can derail the person's destiny. It can be a recipe for failure, ego, and harm to God's people. We now have Jesus as our blueprint for anointed ministry.

Jesus was anointed with the Spirit of God and with power (Acts 10:38) for the special ministry appointed to Him. When He was baptised, He was filled with the Holy Spirit (Luke 4). He *only* did the work of the Father, listening carefully to His voice and direction through the Spirit:

> *The Spirit of the* LORD *is upon Me,*
> *Because He has anointed Me*
> *To preach the gospel to the poor;*
> *He has sent Me to heal the brokenhearted,*
> *To proclaim liberty to the captives*
> *And recovery of sight to the blind,*
> *To set at liberty those who are oppressed;*
> *To proclaim the acceptable year of the* LORD.
> (Luke 4:18–19, quoted from Isaiah)

We cannot go wrong if we follow His blueprint for our life and worship! So why is this so difficult? Probably because the hardest sacrifice is where we give ourselves over to the power and direction of the Spirit of Jesus. It's a risk of Christianity to think we can get by with a bunch of Jesus' words in our heads. And even when we allow some of those words to penetrate our hearts, how difficult is it to walk them out every day?

This chapter might have felt like a punch in the head! If so, I pray you will recover from your temporary concussion and allow the words to challenge your belief system. God hasn't changed. We must. But know this: His fire is a welcoming and warm blaze to those who make Him their shelter. From this place, His fire will not damage you. It will heal and sustain you, burning out the stubborn mildew in your life, and prepare you for glory.

It's a risk of Christianity to think we can get by with a bunch of Jesus' words in our heads.

13

Stuck on the Threshold

We cannot cross over into promise if we don't trust God. We don't have the faith for it. The Jordan is an insurmountable barrier, and we don't understand why we need to cross it. We worry about whether God will look after us on this side, so we keep Him at a distance. We fear the giants on the other side, so we refuse to move from the wilderness (Numbers 13 and 14).

A wilderness mentality can kill your destiny. I am referring to your purpose and destiny here on Earth, whatever this looks like for us as individuals. For all of us, however, it involves supporting the establishment of God's spiritual kingdom on earth in the 'now.' We too can choose to struggle against the will and word of God, or we can yield in obedience and hasten into the Spirit's realm.

Crossing the Jordan speaks of triumph. There is much more to do on the other side, but God has declared victory. We move into that victory, empowered by the Spirit of God and trusting Him to keep His word. The sad reality is that not everyone will cross the Jordan. The old generation of Israelites remained stuck on the threshold because they never lost their captive mentality. After years of captivity, they were free, but not in their minds. They continually struggled against the new 'yoke' of God.

The Face of Logic

We cannot use pure logic and our reasoning to push through into promise. We must have faith. Faith is the only ingredient humble enough, courageous enough, and radical enough to pursue God's purposes. If His purposes looked like human rationale, we wouldn't require faith because they would seem possible! The returning spies sent to investigate the Promised Land came back with a mixed review. We see here an acknowledgement of God's truth with a big 'but' applied (Numbers 13:31).

God set up the timing for the spies to assess the land of Canaan. He wanted them to see it truly was a land of Promise. He sent them at the beginning of the season for grapes (Numbers 13:20), knowing the bountiful fruit would impress them. The twelve spies definitely found attractive and very large fruit. We are told they cut a branch from a grapevine, and it took two of them to carry one cluster of grapes hanging from it (13:23)!

When the spies returned, they acknowledged the land 'truly flows with milk and honey' (13:27). At that point, they have just verified God's words. They have found His word to be true. Besides the milk and honey, there was the gigantic fruit evidence, revealing the principle that God gives abundantly (see John 10:10).

However, the focus soon shifted to the impossibility of taking land from extra-large people. They were quite happy to take extra-large grapes, pomegranates, and figs, but between them and the fruit were a vast array of physically superior people who owned the fruit. Some of these people were XXL (extra, extra-large). These were offspring of the giants.

Caleb attempted to bring a holy hush to the group as he championed the plan to take possession of their promised inheritance. But Israel wept and wailed. This dramatic episode includes the familiar complaint against Moses with Aaron now included, but with a new dimension added, 'If only we had died in this wilderness!' (Numbers 14:2). How things have changed! Even the challenging wilderness is a preferable place to die. Just the thought of Canaanite swords had them cowering and wailing. The petulant group wanted to return to Egypt under a new leader (14:4). As far as they were concerned, this Promise thing was a lost cause.

The giants had already won the battle over their minds. Let's consider the fact most of these wailing and complaining Israelites had not even seen the giants, which reveals the danger of believing hearsay and opening the door to fear. Rebellion was the big sin in the camp, by not believing the Lord or obeying His command to possess the land (Deuteronomy 9:23–24). The people were so adamant they would not risk their lives in this milk and honey trap that when Joshua and Caleb tore their clothes in despair and exhorted them to believe God at His word, they planned to stone them. (*We* would never do that, right?)

The giants had already won the battle over their minds.

Centuries later, sadly, the stiff neck of pride and religion would still not bow after the Holy Spirit swept through Jerusalem after Pentecost with signs and wonders. Stephen was the first Jesus martyr, stoned to death by some angry descendants of Israel. His crime?

He was too radical in his faith. Stephen had this to say to his fellow Jews, who refused to listen to the message of their Messiah:

> *You stubborn people! You are heathen at heart and deaf to the truth. Must you forever resist the Holy Spirit? That's what your ancestors did, and so do you! Name one prophet your ancestors didn't persecute! They even killed the ones who predicted the coming of the Righteous One—the Messiah whom you betrayed and murdered. You deliberately disobeyed God's law, even though you received it from the hands of angels.* (Acts 7:51–53 NLT)

The New King James Version puts verse 51 this way:

> *You stiff-necked and uncircumcised in heart and ears! You always resist the Holy Spirit; as your fathers did, so do you.*

Stephen hit the nail on the head when he described their behaviour as resistant to the Holy Spirit. If we are resistant to the Holy Spirit, we are being stiff-necked too! Let's take this word seriously and ask for open hearts and spiritual ears. Now, let me put this into some uncomfortable perspective for us today…

It is easy to boo-hoo the Israelites' behaviour, but how often do we, the believing church, engage in such faithless and self-righteous acts? When doubt enters the church, the church loses. She loses her faith. When she loses her faith, she becomes powerless. Let's replay this scene from Numbers in some modern contexts, shall we?

First, there's the subtle, cloaked spiritual response:

> Yes, Caleb, we have seen the fruit of the Spirit. We agree it is good, but we cannot risk the peace of our church congregation

with what you are suggesting. We have a duty to our church and its members, Caleb. Look, we've spent years building this church and don't want to risk what we have. Maybe God doesn't want us to pursue this with all the obstruction we are getting? Yes, Caleb, we are praying about it!

There also could be overt hostility in the name of religious zeal:

Joshua and Caleb are dangerous! Watch out for their deception. If you follow them, you will end up with all kinds of strange beliefs. They actually believe they have the power to defy nature. How dare they suggest we are the rebellious ones, standing up and thinking they have something special we don't have. We believe in the Bible. How dare they suggest we have no faith! Their radical beliefs are toxic. Send them out and tell the congregation to have nothing to do with them!

Perhaps this is the modern equivalent of a good stoning? Giving a good tongue lashing and an excommunication for good measure may be seen as 'righteous' and keeping the radical element or 'strange fire' at bay. But the Numbers passages tell a different story.

If we are resistant to the Holy Spirit, we are being stiff-necked too!

Joshua and Caleb were the ones on the Lord's side. The congregation were the ones to lift their voices in logic and reason—bringing their word against God's word.

How often do logic and reason cause a church congregation to miss the faith connection? If it looks logical according to a human decision, then it isn't a matter of faith. Faith stretches and tests you. It tests you immediately for the unbelief in your heart.

Unbelief will prevent you from reaching your full destiny, despite being a child of God. This includes twisting Scripture to suit your narrative. Yes—this happens more than we care to think! Without the Spirit of God removing the religious and rational blindfolds from our eyes, we are in danger of misinterpreting or reinterpreting the word of God. The twisting serpent is forever succeeding in his word-twisting tactic, having experienced its resounding success in the garden; 'Did God *really* say that?' If God says He will give His power to us to do (insert promise here), then if we doubt or refuse to step into it, we are no different from our wailing wilderness examples.

If We're Honest

Maybe we have struggled our way across a wilderness with our spiritual insecurities and trust issues. Maybe we have cried out, 'Are we there yet!?' more times than we care to count or remember because we were discontent with our position. We may have been believers in Jesus for many years, maybe even seeing His miracles, but until now, we've been walking the good Christian route without the full empowering of the Spirit in our lives. We haven't yet fully surrendered and stepped into the full promise of God for our lives because we haven't been ready to face it—or maybe we didn't trust He would deliver on His promise.

While there are rugged beauties to be found in the wilderness and an occasional watering hole with a few palms, it is not a friendly and inviting land. In fact, the Bible refers to it as 'terrible', 'dreadful', and 'terrifying', depending on the version you read (Deuteronomy 1:19, 8:15). Have you ever felt terror on your journey? What about a feeling of dread? Perhaps it is time to stop and reconsider the Lord's word concerning you. Dread and terror are not His gifts to you! If we are a believer in Jesus and experiencing the wilderness, the devil will work overtime to convince us it is our destiny. Don't believe him! The enemy uses dread and terror against our minds to topple the peace and confidence of the word of God. We require big faith!

If His purposes looked like human rationale, we wouldn't require faith, because they would seem possible!

14

Jesus, the Fulfilment

Do not think that I came to destroy the Law or the Prophets. I did not come to destroy but to fulfill.
— Jesus (Matthew 5:17)

We do not step into promise because of our righteousness. The Israelites took possession of their land because of the inhabitants' evil and to fulfil the Lord's word to Abraham, Isaac, and Jacob (Deuteronomy 9:4–6). We are led by the Spirit into our promise, but we haven't earned it. The sacrifice of Jesus Christ makes it possible. When we accept Jesus has done all the work, it privileges us to become part of the family. In a covenant relationship, we can also enjoy the victories and blessings of God.

Fully Filled

Deconstructing the English word fulfil, we find 'full' and 'fill.' There's a point where a container or vessel won't take any more. You can only fill your cup to its brim. If you keep pouring, your cup will overflow. Fullness is a state of being and one we humans don't achieve often.

One area we absolutely fail to come close to being fully filled is righteousness! It is impossible for us in our world-born state to make ourselves righteous. We can be good, but we cannot be the holy perfection of God. The old covenant sacrificial system teaches us it cannot produce a permanent state of righteousness *or* remove the guilt of our sin. It also teaches us holiness is God's requirement, represented in perfect (no blemishes allowed) lambs, goats, and bulls. Our failure at being righteous is the very reason our Redeemer championed our cause on behalf of the Father and submitted to death on a cross. Only He can fully fill the righteousness of God.

When God established the requirements for worship in His Tabernacle, Aaron, as high priest, was the only one able to make the special yearly atonement for the people's sins. He acted as a mediator between God and the people. Bulls and goats were not God's perfect sacrifice but an imperfect substitute until He was ready to reveal His Messiah (Hebrews 10). When Jesus died as the sinless man, He satisfied God's requirements, becoming the once-for-all sacrifice to negate the need for further lambs, bulls, and goats. He ended (fulfilled) the sacrificial system. This is excellent news for us because the blood of bulls and goats doesn't remove sin! And without Jesus, we would still be living in our sinful, guilt-ridden state (ouch).

> *Under the old covenant, the priest stands and ministers before the altar day after day, offering the same sacrifices again and again, which can never take away sins. **But our High Priest offered himself to God as a single sacrifice for sins, good for all time.** Then he sat down in the place of honor at God's right hand. There he waits until his enemies are humbled and made a footstool under his feet. For by that one offering he forever made perfect those who are being made holy.* (Hebrews 10:11–14 NLT, emphasis mine)

The Biggest Role in History

To take on the High Priest's role, Jesus had to meet its requirements and carry out its duties. His primary duty was to make a sacrifice on behalf of everyone who had ever lived or will live. As High Priest, He could not ignore or break the commandments God gave Moses—not even one, and not even in secret. Even a hint of sin would have ended His role as High Priest. Legal perfection was required to become the spotless Lamb of God. Jesus' soul was the substitute for our souls (Isaiah 53:10). His soul couldn't have even a tiny blemish on it.

That is amazing! To live a holy life every second of every day is not something I can comprehend. There were no days when Jesus woke up and said, 'Hey, Dad, I'm not going to work today'. There were no teenage drunken parties or sneaking out of the house at night. Every day of His life, He awoke and said, 'How will I honour my Father today?' And by extension, every day He was saying to us, 'You are on my mind'. His sacrifice was brutal in the end, but He actually sacrificed for us every day of His life by refusing to take His eyes off the end goal. I've met some dedicated and loyal people in my time, but no one comes close to the Son of God.

Sacrifice and offering You did not desire,
But a body You have prepared for Me.
In burnt offerings and sacrifices for sin
You had no pleasure.
Then I said, "Behold, I have come—
In the volume of the book it is written of Me—
To do Your will, O God.
(Hebrews 10:5–7)

Heritage

If Jesus had been born through his earthly father, Joseph, He would have been born into sin because Adam's line birthed sin. As a result, sin and death became our generational heritage (Romans 5:12). The High Priest and Lamb of God could not have brought us into eternal life if death was His spiritual heritage. Jesus had to be supernaturally born of the Spirit to bypass this lineage issue. He had to be a man, like Adam, to make the sacrifice for humans. But He also had to be God because only God can make us perfect.

And so it is written: "The first man Adam became a living being." The last man Adam, became a life-giving spirit.
(1 Corinthians 15:45)

The fact Jesus determined to deny all claim to the benefits of His divinity and walk out life in full humanity is itself a deep mystery. Not once did He use His rights and wave them in someone's face. He laid down all rights and showed us how to die to ourselves; how to overcome our selfish desires. Oh, to have this capacity! (Oh, wait... I can! That's a benefit His death provided me... Jesus, help me!)

Everything God set up for His people points to their Messiah. Jesus is the fulfilment of all of Israel's feasts, and God wants us to celebrate Him, just as the Israelites kept their feasts of honour and remembrance. Over the course of hundreds of years, the prophets of God gave testimony of the Messiah. When Jesus came, He met the criteria for Messiah, including His lineage through Abraham, Isaac, Jacob, and David, and His promised birth in Bethlehem (Micah 5:2). Matthew 1 is, therefore, not a waste of time to read! It is a very intentional introduction to establish Jesus as Messiah.

The concept of heritage would be key for the post wilderness generations of Israel. The nations of the Earth had their gods, gods established outside of the Creator's will during the troubled times of

Nimrod, Babel, and the great turning away (Genesis 6–11). The story of Abraham is, therefore, a story of God selecting a nation for Himself to re-establish His name in the Earth. His first Adam did not produce life for others, but His second Adam would renew the covenant between God and humans.

Abraham was a type of new Adam because, from Him, a nation dedicated to the one true God would be born. From one chosen nation, the light would spread to other nations. Kings of the earth like Alexander the Great have conquered nations and put them under subjection. *Our* King reveals His continual desire for free and willing relationship, not subjection. He invites us to join Him.

Priest and King

It is from this place of heritage the prophecies take place. They proclaim a new lineage and new life branching from it. The tree of death would be cut off, and the tree of life will branch out into all the people groups of planet Earth.

Jesus is identified as being of the priestly order of Melchizedek, who was both priest and king (Hebrews 5 and 7). Jesus could *not* be of the Levite line to mediate the new covenant because God could not use the imperfect nature of the Mosaic covenant to fulfil His perfect covenant. Instead, He chose a new lineage through Judah and a royal one at that! Lineage was important to the Israelites and their descendants. There is an excellent reason! God promised them a Messiah and told them where to look in the family tree. The new Priest-King would be birthed from the old royal lineage and fulfil God's promise to David (1 Chronicles 17).

> *Out of the stump of David's family will grow a shoot—*
> *yes, a new **Branch** bearing fruit from the old root.*

*And the Spirit of the LORD will rest on him—
the Spirit of wisdom and understanding,
the Spirit of counsel and might,
the Spirit of knowledge and the fear of the LORD.*
(Isaiah 11:1–2 NLT, emphasis mine)

This Branch of David's line would also walk in the Spirit of wisdom and bring justice against the enemies of God, striking the earth with the 'rod of His mouth' (Isaiah 11:4).

When Jesus was crucified, He died as both priest and king. We are familiar with the mocking that accompanied Jesus' punishment and death. But despite the enemy's mocking voice deriding Jesus as King of the Jews, the confronting sign above His head revealed the *truth* of who He was. In the heavenly realms and on Earth, the High Priest was fulfilling His duty, and a forever King was declared.

The first high priest of Israel was Aaron. He made atonement once a year for the sin of his people, entering the Holy of Holies according to specific requirements. This day was very important! To perform his duties, Aaron had to wear holy linen garments that were not to be worn for general priestly use. When he finished his elaborate set of sacrifices, Aaron had to take off the linen garments and leave them outside the Holy of Holies.

To fulfil both law and prophecies, Jesus reveals Himself to His people as High Priest in overt and subtle ways. As Lamb of God, He was overt in His duties. But note the subtlety related to the garments He wore in death (the following Scripture refers to Joseph of Arimathea, who took Jesus' body down from the cross and laid it in His own unused tomb).

*When Joseph had taken the body, he wrapped it in a **clean linen cloth**...* (Matthew 27:59, emphasis mine).

In death, Jesus made His sacrifice before His Father, wearing clean linen garments in the obedient pattern of Israel's High Priest. What did Jesus do when He rose from the dead? He did exactly what Aaron would have done after completing the atonement sacrifice in the Holy of Holies. He took off the linen garments—and He left them in the tomb. His sacrificial business as High Priest was complete. Personally, I find this detail exciting! It's so specific and tells me our God crafted His redemption plan in the finest of detail.

Time in Egypt

Jesus not only fulfilled the law and prophets, His physical journey on Earth modelled that of Israel. It was prophesied Jesus would also be called out of Egypt (Hosea 11:1). When King Herod heard about the birth of Jesus from the Magi, he gave the dreadful orders to kill all boys in Bethlehem two years old and younger. God warned Jesus' earthly father, Joseph, in a dream and told him to escape to Egypt with Mary and Jesus so the child would be safe (Matthew 2). Jesus lived in Egypt until Herod died, and God again spoke to Joseph in a dream, this time telling him it was safe for the family to return to Israel. His time in Egypt mirrors the time spent by His ancestors there.

One of Jesus' most famous ancestors was the vizier to Pharoah during the time of the great famine that caused Jacob and his family to migrate to Egypt. Both Jesus and Joseph were betrayed by their brothers, those of their lineage and spiritual heritage. And both ended up in Egypt because of someone else's evil intentions towards them. But God's plan was not thwarted.

Joseph's life provides a beautiful picture of the Messiah as Bread of Life—our sustenance. He was planted in Egypt via unusual circumstances in readiness to provide for his family in a time of famine. When Joseph was raised up as vizier, he fed the hungry masses from his abundant kingdom store-house reserves. It was Joseph who planned these reserves, using Pharaoh's finances to do so. Pharaoh gave all power and authority to Joseph to feed the hungry (Genesis 41).

When God sent His Son to Earth, He gave Him all power and authority to lay down His life (John 10:17–18). In death, God raised Jesus on the cross to draw the spiritually hungry to Him, feeding them from the inexhaustible spiritual storehouses of Father God. He then raised Him to life, empowering His work. Note the pattern in Scripture is first the natural and then the spiritual (1 Corinthians 15:46).

Joseph was called into a position to provide for his family, God's chosen people, but he also saved Egypt and the nations of the world (Genesis 41 and 42). Jesus reveals the pattern of the gospel in Acts 1:8, feeding his family first (the Jews), then distant relatives (the Samaritans), and finally the nations (ends of the earth). Like a pebble thrown into a pond, the ripples move outward from a central point. God's plan is to spread His love and salvation across the globe, but He starts with family.

God raised Jesus on the cross to draw the spiritually hungry to Him, feeding them from the inexhaustible spiritual storehouses of Father God.

The Tabernacle of Hope

We are also woven into the pages of Scripture, many centuries before we were born! The Tabernacle of God, built and assembled in the wilderness, was a physical representation of God living with people.

The Israelites could experience God through sacrifice and worship within an intricately decorated tent and courtyard and using tangible heavenly models. But the Messiah, while present, was hidden from their spiritual eyes.

Instead of God living with people,
He now lives in people.

Messiah is reflected in the pure oil and continual light of the Tabernacle's lampstand. His fragrance is found in the incense offered up each day, the pleasing offering to soothe God's wrath towards us because of our sin. The delight of the incense contrasts sharply with the gruesome representation of the veil across the Holy of Holies. This veil was torn in two, representing Jesus' body, torn to make a way for us to come into God's presence (Hebrews 10:20).

The washbasin of cleansing reminds us of the cleansing we receive through Christ, who purifies us so we can commune with God. And the anointing oil used to consecrate the Tabernacle articles made everything holy, including the priests. This precious oil reminds us of the Holy Spirit, who anoints nothing not anointed by God through Jesus. The oil was not to be recreated outside its holy use and was not for personal use. Neither is the anointing of the Holy Spirit. It exists for God's use alone.

As the pattern of Scripture has revealed, first stands the natural, and then comes the spiritual. The Tabernacle of the Israelites was a temporary Tent of Meeting and worship. The body of Christ now forms the Tabernacle of God on Earth, but the transient nature of this tent remains. Instead of God living with people, He now lives in people. The anointing of God's Spirit empowers us as a community because the work of Jesus is no longer externalised. Now, the Light of the Tabernacle shines within us, doing a deep work of sanctification and illuminating our minds and hearts. From that place, His Tabernacle takes His light to the world.

Our Portion

From amongst the sacrifices presented at the Tabernacle, portions were allocated to the priests, reflecting God was their portion, and they relied on Him for their needs. As the holy priesthood of believers, Jesus has become our portion. When we look at how God divides the portions, we must realise He has heaped our plates full! The provision of Jesus was full and complete. As Bread of Life, Living Water, Healer, Provider, Comforter, and all His many other names and attributes, He truly provides for every one of our human needs. He waits for us to feast at His bountiful table and enjoy His goodness. Will you join Him?

We will never exhaust the detail of the Messiah within the pages of Scripture. Jesus is found everywhere because He is the substance of life that holds us together (Colossians 1:16). His fulfilment of law and prophecy provides for our fulfilment. Righteousness is no longer impossible because our great High Priest made a complete sacrifice on our behalf. I rejoice because I'm covered with His breastplate of righteousness (Ephesians 6:14) and sustained through His life-giving substance. As I leave more of myself behind, there is more room for Him in my life.

God designed you as a vessel for His glory, and your personal contentment and fulfilment is reliant on being fully filled with His presence and power. From this place of fulfilment, your spiritual gifts and callings flow. You, too, have been called out of Egypt and into the glorious inheritance of promise.

He waits for us to feast at His bountiful table and enjoy His goodness. Will you join Him?

15

A New Generation

I liken the Jordan River crossing to when I crossed over from my striving and religious beliefs into the freedom of life in the Spirit. Like the Israelites, this process took me close to forty years! The concept of going from one camp to another and repeating the same daily and weekly cycles is familiar and exhausting. Like the Israelites, I couldn't really hear what God was saying in a deep spiritual sense. I tried to do what was right, but I wasn't entirely confident in God's ability to carry out 'my' plans. Sadly, I didn't believe He had the best for me, so I trekked a few unnecessary wilderness paths and lost a few years. (I am extremely grateful He is a God of restoration who can redeem those years for me.)

Religion had taught me God carried a stick, and the journey was always difficult. The irony of this book is it was the Israelites' story that supported the melding of this view into my belief system. I saw God as having a stick and punishing His children. It is only now that I have walked across my own Jordan I can look back and view the Israelites' wilderness journey as it actually occurred. Now I see a merciful and patient God! I see a group who were rebellious and intent on tripping themselves up. If God couldn't tell them, who could?

They literally took their free will and shook it at God. They desired rescue without a relationship.

The Handover

Before Moses died and formally handed the people over to Joshua's leadership, he gave the new generation of Israel a full recap of how God had delivered them, and he covered all God's requirements for societal and holy living. Don't we need reminding of God's word regularly? The word of God encouraged and warned this generation before moving into their inheritance. In fact, Moses wrote a song on God's instruction and taught it to the people. Sadly, the song eventually became a witness against them when they strayed from God's commandments (Deuteronomy 31 and 32). But on this occasion, the people listened to Moses and renewed God's covenant in readiness for their new life.

When we are about to face a large and apparently superior enemy, we must seek reassurance from the word of God and take hold of its promises with courage.

Joshua was selected to take the children of Israel from the wilderness to Promise, so Moses commissioned him in front of the people. Moses also commanded Joshua to be strong and of good courage. He knew from experience Joshua would need as much strength and courage as he could get. These people needed strong leadership to defeat the enemy and get settled into their Promised Land.

> *So be strong and courageous! Do not be afraid and do not panic before them. For the LORD your God will personally go ahead of you. He will neither fail you nor abandon you.* (Deuteronomy 31:6 NLT)

Joshua travelled the wilderness for an additional thirty-eight years he did not deserve. Sometimes we suffer because our people group is misaligned with God's word. However, God does not waste time as we do! Joshua spent time as an apprentice under Moses. He learned to be faithful, and he lived humbly, never taking Moses on for leadership as others tried to do.

When Moses died, God reminded Joshua to take hold of strength and courage to defeat the enemy. When we are about to face a large and apparently superior enemy, we must seek reassurance from the word of God and take hold of its promises with courage. Joshua took hold of God's word and immediately put it into action.

The Man Joshua

Joshua was the one patiently waiting for Moses on the mountainside when Moses received the Ten Commandments from the Lord. He was the servant who remained behind at the Tent of Meeting, preferring to soak in the presence of God that lingered there rather than hurry off 'home.'

Joshua's faithfulness is an extraordinary testimony. He was one of the twelve spies, first tasked to go into Canaan and spy out this pleasant land (Numbers 13). He and Caleb almost lost their lives because the people refused to listen and take their inheritance, preferring instead to give in to fear and remain in the wilderness (Numbers 14). God rewarded Joshua's faithfulness, along with Caleb, with divine strength even in old age. The mantle of Moses' leadership fell to Joshua. It's a testament to this man that the people of Israel accepted him as they accepted Moses, and until his death, they served the Lord (Joshua 24:31).

Joshua is also a type of Jesus (we can discover more of this in the Hebrew meaning of their names). He marked the transition from old to new life. This does not denigrate Moses! Moses was the man for the wilderness job. He was the mighty prophet and mediator of the first covenant. While God refused Moses entry into Canaan because of a failure on his behalf, there is something prophetic in the fact the old covenant representative could not lead the people into new territory. Instead, we have a Jesus-type in Joshua to take the people into their inheritance. It is the work of Jesus to take us across the unpassable chasm from our sinful state into a relationship with His Father. Jesus *is* the crossing.

Joshua, freshly anointed with the spirit of wisdom (Deuteronomy 34:9), rallies the tribes for their transition into Promise. He calls for consecration of the people, just as Moses did before God gave the commandments at Mount Sinai. He also tells them that within three days, they would cross over into Canaan (Joshua 1:11). This is a prophetic glimpse of the death, burial, and resurrection of Jesus. The people would receive their new life of Promise on the third day!

Jesus is the crossing.

Unlike the first time the Israelites took a peek into enemy territory, this time, they would succeed. Freshly reminded of the Lord's word, Joshua prepared them for the pivotal event that had eluded them for forty years. It was time to cross over.

16

Crossing Over (finally)!

The generation of the men of war baptised in the Red Sea was now dead. This new generation had not experienced baptism. Again, God takes them through a transition into new life. But this time, it's their final destination point! This time, they know who God is as they walk in obedience, not fear. They are ready to take Him at His word and make the transition from wilderness to Promise.

I love how the people of this generation get their own crossing story! They had heard about the Red Sea miracle but had not experienced it. Now, with their own eyes, they witness something similar.

Another Baptism

Jordan, or *Yarden* from the Hebrew, means to descend or to flow down.[1] It's a perfect name for a river! But Jordan provides a spiritual picture of God's love flowing down from heaven. Jordan is also where Jesus stood years later, receiving the anointing for His ministry as the heavens opened and the Spirit of God came upon Him (Matthew 3).

It was *always* God's plan to send heaven to Earth in the form of His Son.

This historic crossing was not a slap-dash affair! It had holy significance. The priests were instructed to enter Jordan ahead of all the people with the Ark of the Testimony raised on their shoulders. The ark provides a picture of Jesus, in honour and with authority, lifted up and going first into Promise. Jesus goes before us in everything and leads us across the chasm of separation from God into our glorious inheritance. As we understand the holy nature of the ark, we see why there were strict observances for handling it.

It is our privilege as the priesthood of Jesus to bear His burden as ministers of the gospel.

The ark resided in the Holy of Holies and contained manna in a gold pot, Aaron's budding rod, and the commandments (Hebrews 9:3–4). Each item represented Jesus as the Bread of Life, the authority of God, and the Word of God. Above the ark were cherubim of glory, overshadowing the mercy seat where Jesus' blood now speaks for us (Hebrews 9:5, 12:22–24).

There is authority where the priesthood of Messiah treads! When the feet of the priests touched the water, God caused the Jordan River's flow to be cut off (Joshua 3:13). Now standing on the *dry* riverbed, the priests carefully positioned themselves with the ark and waited until all the children of Israel had crossed. Only when every man, woman, and child had hurried across the riverbed did the priests follow. Standing in the Jordan, the burden of Christ was literally on the shoulders of this priesthood. They 'bore' the ark 'until they finished everything the Lord had commanded Joshua' (Joshua 4:10). It is our privilege as the priesthood of Jesus to bear His burden as ministers of the gospel. But unlike the world's burden, His burden is light (Matthew 11:30).

I feel like we need a drum roll at this point. Or a shofar blast! Abraham's numerous descendants were now in their Promised Land! A centuries-old Promise had come true.

The Army of God

The second baptism of Israel was profoundly different than the first. The first baptism was for a group of captives fleeing from enemy territory. This group of ex-slaves was in a defensive position and needed a rescue. Their first baptism destroyed the enemy in their lives. This second baptism prophetically declared new life in Christ. It saw a refined group of God-followers confidently heading into enemy territory. They were on the offensive! The wilderness period had turned a group of wailing wanderers into warriors.

It is impossible to fight a powerful enemy with a meat pot mentality.

Scripture tells us the location selected for crossing the Jordan was directly opposite Jericho (Joshua 3:16). Jericho was a powerful and fortified enemy city. This was an overt declaration of war! God identified Jericho as the first conquest for this new warrior nation.

When we step into the power of the Spirit, the enemy gets worried. He needs to because God is about to carry out His word. The children of Israel have developed into a big, organised army ready for a righteous fight! God's plan to bring judgement to Canaan was being fulfilled. His army was ready, and His royal standard (the ark) had been raised.

It is only through the empowering of the Spirit of Christ we turn from frightened ex-captives into confident warriors. If you resonate with a frightened captive more than a confident warrior, it's time to build a relationship with the Promised One…

The Promised One

The second baptism of the children of Israel has prophetic overtones of the baptism of the Holy Spirit (Matthew 3, Luke 3, and Acts 2). This new baptism provides us with the empowerment of Christ. It is the work of Christ to both cleanse *and* fill. We must be cleansed for a relationship with God. We must be *filled* to operate in His authority. It is impossible to fight a powerful enemy with a meat pot mentality. We must learn to be spiritual conquerors, moving from wilderness survival mentality to soldier mentality (promise).

Jesus describes the Holy Spirit as the Promise of His Father. He made it clear to His disciples that the Holy Spirit was to be desired, even telling them it was better He (Jesus) leave them so the Helper (Spirit) could come to them (John 16:7). The Amplified version expands on Helper to include Comforter, Advocate, Intercessor/Counsellor, Strengthener, and Standby. This list helps us understand the high value of the Holy Spirit for our faith walk.

If Jesus emphasised the Spirit so strongly, He must be very important.

*Listen carefully: I am sending **the Promise of My Father** [the Holy Spirit] upon you; but you are to remain in the city [of*

Jerusalem] until you are clothed (fully equipped) with power from on high. (Luke 24:49 AMP, emphasis mine)

The role of the Holy Spirit includes equipping His church with the power of God. It is no longer just one special tribe that ministers to the Lord. As believers in Jesus, we are members of a new holy priesthood, empowered by God to do signs and wonders and witness the transformation of lives for the kingdom. The Spirit equips the true church with gifts for Jesus' ministry on Earth. But we administer them from the position of laid-down lives.

To understand what a laid-down life looks like, we can examine Israel's priesthood. The Levites were called to lay down their personal desires to obey the calling on their life. They had to trust God, even for their food. There was no room for self-sufficiency when the congregation of Israel provided for all their physical needs. They had to come before God humbly, trusting that every day the system He set up for their wellbeing would provide for them and their families. A Spirit-led life is sometimes an uncertain one! It is a journey we must take in faith.

As believers in Jesus, we are members of a new holy priesthood, empowered by God to do signs and wonders and witness the transformation of lives for the kingdom.

A Combined Work

Jesus and the Spirit always work in harmony and are firmly united. This was the pattern throughout Jesus' ministry on Earth. We have a beautiful and unusual picture of the Spirit and the Lamb working together in the consecration of Aaron and his sons (Exodus 28–29). We see the combined work of Jesus and the Holy Spirit represented in the blood sprinkled on Aaron and the oil poured over his head.

What a sight! Blood spattered Aaron's fresh and beautifully constructed garments, while oil flowed freely down his beard and clothing (Psalm 133). He was cleansed by the blood and anointed for service by the oil. This was no accidental picture. Many years later, Jesus the Messiah, covered in His own blood and flowing freely with the anointing of the Spirit, entered the holy place in heaven before His Father and presented Himself as the sacrifice for all sin. Jesus is the *fulfilment* of the Levite ministry.

All true ministry is done through the unified work of Spirit and Son because this is the pattern of heaven. Without Jesus, there is no atonement for sin, and without the Spirit, there is no empowerment to live the new life promised to us. The apostle Peter provides an excellent example of why we need the Spirit in our lives. This faithful man walked with Messiah, learning His ways firsthand. He even cast out demons and healed the sick. But it was not until the Day of Pentecost, when the Spirit swept through that upper room, that Peter became 'the rock', and birthed the church of Jesus Christ through his anointed preaching (Acts 2).

Our Guarantee

When I think of the Israelites crossing over into Promise, I recognise Jesus made their way possible. It is only through Jesus we can be freed from bondage and develop a relationship with the Father. However, I see the new life in Canaan as similar to the life of the Spirit. There is a greater level of victory as we learn it's by supernatural faith we can move mountains, slay giants, and bring the reality of heaven to Earth.

We have moved past the stage where we learn by rote and the awkward teen years of our spirituality, where we may question our identity and faith, and we step into confidence in the word of God and, by extension, the Person of God.

> *And when you believed in Christ, he identified you as his own by giving you the Holy Spirit, whom he promised long ago. The Spirit is God's guarantee that he will give us the inheritance he promised and that he has purchased us to be his own people.* (Ephesians 1:13–14 NLT)

The perfect and much-needed Holy Spirit is a guarantee of our future inheritance. We cannot simply be followers of Jesus. The wilderness story is a clear testimony to this. Only believers in Jesus can move into promise. We must have the Spirit of God to cross over into the newness of life. It is not enough to title yourself a 'Christian' or a 'disciple'. You must believe in your heart God raised Jesus from the dead and let it flow out as a declaration of your allegiance to Jesus as Lord (Romans 10:9).

We need a greater measure of God, a deeper relationship that removes all fear and births the signs and wonders of God in our lives. Faith in Jesus is meant to be exciting!

> *And these signs will follow those who believe: In My name they will cast out demons; they will speak with new tongues; they will take up serpents; and if they drink anything deadly, it will by no means hurt them; they will lay hands on the sick, and they will recover.* (Mark 16:17–18)

17

Mt Gerizim and Mt Ebal

Be strong and very courageous. Be careful to obey all the instructions Moses gave you. Do not deviate from them, turning either to the right or to the left. Then you will be successful in everything you do. Study this Book of Instruction continually. Meditate on it day and night so you will be sure to obey everything written in it. Only then will you prosper and succeed in all you do. This is my command—be strong and courageous! Do not be afraid or discouraged. For the Lord your God is with you wherever you go. (Joshua 1:7–9 NLT)

Moses was careful to review the whole law of God with the people of Israel before they entered Canaan. He knew their success (blessing) depended on their obedience. That was how the God of Israel operated. Obedience to His word brought blessing. Disobedience brought the opposite—curses. Curses included disease, such as the plagues that came when Israel sinned and also the humiliation of defeat by their enemies. Just before Moses died, he instructed the people to do something unusual. When they entered the land of Promise, they were to stand on the mountains of Gerizim and Ebal to pronounce blessings and curses over themselves (Deuteronomy 27). Now that is not an everyday occurrence!

After crossing the Jordan, Joshua obeyed God's word to the letter, setting the people up for their success. First, they erected memorial stones as instructed. Then the new generation was circumcised. Afterwards, they set up an altar according to Moses' instruction, made of uncut stones and having the law of God inscribed into it. The people sacrificed to their God and celebrated, giving thanks to Him for their arrival and His goodness. Their altar now stood as a testament to the God of Abraham, Isaac, and Jacob in a land that worshipped other gods. They were in the land of Promise! What a celebration that must have been.

But before the big clean-out of Canaan, the children of Israel obeyed Moses' somewhat unusual instruction to pronounce specific blessings and curses from the tops of the two mountains. Half the tribes were to stand on Mount Gerizim (Simeon, Levi, Judah, Issachar, Joseph, and Benjamin). These tribes would bless the people. The remaining tribes of Reuben, Gad, Asher, Zebulun, Dan, and Naphtali were to stand on the opposing Mount Ebal and declare the curses for disobedience.

Under the Curse

The Israelites were entering the pointy end of re-affirming the covenant by declaring curses over themselves. They were effectively standing before God and saying, 'Yes, Lord, if we do this sin, then we will receive the assigned punishment'. Blessings are easy to receive! I wonder if they really understood the magnitude of their agreement. It would appear later generations did not. There is more detail about curses in Deuteronomy (27–28) than of blessings. This tells me the Lord did not leave His people guessing on this important matter. He wanted them to receive the blessings and avoid the curses.

The declaration of blessing covered crops, children, herds and their offspring, food, and comforts. We read of a blessing for victory over enemies and another for Israel as a leader of nations. There is the promise of rain in season, the prosperity of produce, and food in the storehouses. The blessings were physical in nature and provided fully for the safety, security, and comforts of God's people. God was clear to let the people know of His desire to bless them. Their end of the covenant was to walk in obedience to their God. He would provide for their food, their health, and child-bearing and give them long life:

So you shall serve the Lord your God, and He will bless your bread and your water. And I will take sickness away from the midst of you. No one shall suffer miscarriage or be barren in your land; I will fulfill the number of your days.
(Exodus 23:25–26)

The remaining curses caused the opposite. If Israel pulled away from obedience and particularly if she flirted with and worshipped other gods under this covenant, the Lord God was not required to continue to bless them. Not only would the blessing disappear, but curses would take their place. It would be deliberate on her behalf, as surely as if she had slammed the door on God and returned to Egypt. This meant the people could expect lack, plague, and sickness of every description, confusion, defeat by their enemies, mildew to destroy their crops, and finally when things became awful—captivity.

While God's blessings take up a few paragraphs, the curses take up most of Moses' monologue. The detail includes sores, boils, fever, and inflammation, along with locusts eating their produce and olives that drop off the trees. Mental illness will also descend upon the nation. Most painfully, the children would be taken captive. (Consider reading Deuteronomy 28 to get the breadth and depth of the curses proclaimed.)

> *God was clear to let the people know of His desire to bless them.*

In this context, curses were punishment for breaking particular laws of God, just like any nation on Earth has laws and punishment for breaking them in its justice system. God set up a justice system for this new nation in the making and meticulously spelled out the consequences of lack of obedience towards his laws. He gave His people so much detail that when the time arrived, they would know for sure why things went so wrong.

Sparrows and Landing Strips

In the Book of Proverbs, there is a curious verse that says:

> *Like a flitting sparrow, like a flying swallow, so a curse without cause shall not alight.* (Proverbs 26:2)

There is a sense in which a curse 'lands.' At Mount Ebal, we see the clear connection between disobedience and curses landing. Disobedience against God's laws is the 'cause'. How many of *us* leave a landing strip open in our lives for a curse to land? We need to shut down that airstrip!

God will not share His throne and worship, and He has a clear expectation we will obey His word. Health, prosperity, and peace—aren't they what most people want today? Well, Israel had it. God withheld nothing from His children. But, when the people stopped taking His word seriously a few generations later, the curses came just as God had said. Law has a double edge. Unfortunately, as we can see through the writings of God's prophets, the answer was simple—repent! But Jeremiah's experience reveals that pride overrode this simple exercise in humility. The consequences were catastrophic.

The Nature of Curses

Blessings and curses did not arrive with the Israelites and the Mosaic covenant. Blessings and curses are principles of God's law we first see in the opening chapters of Genesis. The somewhat uncomfortable reality is God was the originator of the first curse (Genesis 3). But it is comforting to know He will also be the destroyer of all curses. The bookends of Scripture tell me exactly how and why a curse entered the world and when and why a curse will exit the world.

Curse entered because humans did not obey God. When sin has been judged, and Death is finally destroyed, there will be no more curse (Revelation 20 and 22). This reveals the direct connection between curse and sin. To study blessings and curses is to realise their connection between obedience and disobedience and, therefore, life and death. Blessings are the outcome of obedience and produce life. Curses are the outcome of disobedience and produce death. Blessings are connected to fruitfulness and plenty, while curses are connected to barrenness and lack. And curses can be generational (Exodus 34:7, Numbers 14:18).

The first chapter of Genesis tells me God is a God of blessing. When God blessed His creation, He made a direct connection to fruitfulness, which is a somewhat spiritual way of describing increase and abundance. He blessed both animals and humans with the ability to recreate, and this process was designed to be fulfilling and perfect. There was a condition to this blissful state of being: 'Of every tree of the garden you may freely eat; but of the tree of the knowledge of good and evil you shall not eat, for in the day that you eat of it you shall surely die' (Genesis 2:16–17).

Blessings are the outcome of obedience and produce life. Curses are the outcome of disobedience and produce death.

When Man and Woman disobeyed God's direct (and only) commandment, they instantly felt the impact. Both felt the choking blanket of spiritual death. Suddenly, they knew what lack was. The perfect couple immediately felt shame, which is linked to feelings of worthlessness. Just moments earlier, their complete being was wrapped up in God's life. Painfully, they felt the rift immediately and knew in their new state of disobedience to God's law; that they were no longer worthy.

In the Genesis story, we learn it was Satan in the form of a serpent that brought the temptation, but it was God the Creator who brought the curse. Curse was the consequence of disobedience, and it came against abundance, fruitfulness, and plenty. Adam then had to strive for his food in an agricultural context that rapidly changed from low maintenance to hard ground and a fight against weeds that choked the life out of healthy crops. The spiritual reality of life struggling against death is now seen in every area of our creative existence. Life is such a fight!

Tragically, curse came against the life humans would produce (Genesis 3:16). Pregnancy and childbirth would become difficult. As a woman, I find this confronting. Instead of producing children from a place of pure blessing, Woman would multiply sorrow, and she would experience pain bringing her children into the world. Instead of finding her worth in her Creator, she would seek her worth and identity from her husband, and this would fail. This state of existence came after Man and Woman disobeyed God's law. It was not God's original design for a relationship.

God also cursed the animal kingdom He had made. How that must have broken His Creator's heart! He cursed the cooperating serpent 'more' than the other creatures He had made (Genesis 3:14). Finally, His own Son would be impacted by the curse. The enmity between Satan and Woman (Genesis 3:15) would culminate in the bruising of the Son of Man at Calvary.

Death is the ultimate curse to plague humanity. To reveal the message of the Messiah to a dying world, God formed a nation through Abraham to nurture and model salvation's promise. The Mosaic covenant, with its specific conditions, was for a limited time to guard the sons and daughters of Promise until their Messiah arrived (Galatians 3:23–24).

While I deal with the difficult topic of curses, I want to make it clear that God hates to see His precious creation suffering under the consequence of sin. Hang in there! We will look at His solution more closely in the next chapter.

Being a Fig-Leaf Christian

Before Man and Woman experienced the impact of these curses in their lives, they experienced the distressing bondage of shame. I cannot imagine how painful that day was when their spiritual eyes were indeed open to the reality of evil. They had been clothed with God's glory, and as they walked around the garden, they represented His Tabernacle on Earth. His very breath had filled them with life.

Fig-leaf Christians try to right themselves with a garment of their own making instead of the garment of righteousness Jesus provided.

When the glory left, Man and Woman were exposed. Their nakedness was not only physical, but they had nothing to clothe their inner essence, so they dealt with the outside as best they could by creating a sad garment of fig leaves. How many of us try to deal with the shame of sin and the pain of broken identity with a new hair-do or a set of fashionable clothes? While it's not at all funny, the image appears laughable when we see it for what it is.

When we break God's laws, and our conscience tells us we've sinned, we experience shame. Shame is so uncomfortable that we try to find a solution to make it go away. Of course, it doesn't leave unless we deal with it the proper way—through the cross. Fig-leaf Christians try to right themselves with a garment of their own making instead of the garment of righteousness Jesus provided. But fig leaves make for rather transient garments! Today's costume is tomorrow's compost. So we go around the merry-go-round, stitch ourselves a new costume, and for a short while, we experience a reduction in shame.

Apart from being hopelessly inadequate, the major issue with a fig-leaf garment is God doesn't accept it. Fig leaves represent self-righteousness. And God cannot condone or accept self-righteous acts. By nature, these acts endeavour to make us right before God and replace the priceless garment of righteousness Jesus purchased for us.

Our sin, as mirrored back to us through the law, brings shame. We look at ourselves in its reflection, and we are mortified at our lack. We just do not measure up. But putting on a few fig leaves, whether that means charitable works to feel good about ourselves, a week of self-imposed fasting, or any other outworking, is futile. And it grieves God. We cannot escape curses by hiding behind fig leaves. Man and Woman discovered this the hard way.

The Bible tells us Jesus is the *only* way to have true and abundant life. He is the Curse-breaker. And He also takes away our shame. When your sins have been removed, then your shame has to go too! There is nothing left for it to cling to.

Be Careful. Choose Life.

It is wise to remember God gives us a choice. To the Israelites, He said,

> *I have set before you life and death, the blessing and the curse; therefore, you shall choose life in order that you may live, you and your descendants, by loving the Lord your God, by obeying His voice, and by holding closely to Him; for He is your life [your good life, your abundant life, your fulfillment] and the length of your days, that you may live in the land which the Lord promised [swore] to give to your fathers, to Abraham, Isaac, and Jacob.* (Deuteronomy 30:19–20 AMP, emphasis mine)

People choose curse over blessing for multiple reasons. But ignorance is a big one. Hosea states God's people die through lack of knowledge, and this comes because God's knowledge gets rejected (4:6). Adam and Eve experienced perfect wholeness of mind, body, and spirit when they were in total harmony with their Father. When

God's knowledge was rejected, death arrived on the scene. Do we understand rejecting what God says is serious for our physical, mental, and spiritual health? There is no neutral ground. We also choose death when we live in a spirit of unbelief that refuses to acknowledge the supernatural works of God. You can't enjoy His life when you are blinded by death.

> *It is Father God's deep desire to provide His children with answers and strategies for breakthrough in their lives.*

The spiritual law of life and death remains until the final curtain call, being integrated into both old and new covenants. In many ways, our choices are the same as those of the Israelites. We choose life from the Son of God every day. We choose to live in obedience to His word every day. When we do this, we live in the blessings of God. We will still face hardship, but we have His strength to see us through. Not every difficulty or hardship is because of our sin, but it's worth checking our hearts regularly.

The Corinthian church made the mistake of not taking the Lord's Supper honourably. They literally ate and drank judgement on themselves (1 Corinthians 11). Paul explains to these young believers this was the reason many of them were weak, sick, and had even died. They brought a curse into their midst. How we treat the Son of God still matters. In simple terms, our choices produce life or death outcomes.

It is Father God's deep desire to provide His children with answers and strategies for a breakthrough in their lives. If you ever doubt His goodness towards you, remember the level of detailed planning that went into extracting the children of Israel! It's not His willingness in question. Our God's overwhelming and constant desire is for everyone to have life (John 10:10, 2 Peter 3:9). He does not hide His requirements from us today nor make them complicated to follow. The opposite is true. When we hold on to and honour these principles and patterns of Scripture, we begin to see our breakthrough!

18

The Curse-breaker

Christ has redeemed us from the curse of the law, having become a curse for us (for it is written, "Cursed is everyone who hangs on a tree"), that the blessing of Abraham might come upon the Gentiles in Christ Jesus, that we might receive the promise of the Spirit through faith. (Galatians 3:13–14)

The story of Moses and the children of Israel is an incomplete one because the Messiah had not yet arrived. God provided Jesus and the empowering of the Spirit to bring life, ensuring we have every weapon at our disposal to defeat our inner impulses and remain in a relationship with Him. We don't fear curses of any description because we have the life source of humankind available to us, plugging us back into a relationship with the Father.

It is true we are all born into curse. Does your garden have weeds? Has pain in childbirth vanished? (Not in my experience!) When we say yes to the new life in Jesus, we must remember we are not instantly made perfect. A major spiritual transaction has taken place. But our salvation needs to be walked out daily in the flesh suit that likes to strain against our new life (Romans 7:21–25). We must also apply our new life in a broken world that doesn't recognise the need for God.

Our Blessed Hope!

Every generation of Israelites was born under the curse of the law until Jesus' day. From our study, we now have an image of what 'under the curse of the law' looks like. The children of Israel stood on Mount Ebal and verbally agreed to the curses heaped upon them. Curses would come into effect if they did not continue to do everything written in the law (Galatians 3:10). So *literally*, the children were 'under the curse of the law' by agreeing to its terms. It was a legal contract. If they breached it, they received the associated punishment.

It's a strange thing, but since the time of Jesus, His followers have tried to pin themselves under the stone tablets. This is futile when the New Testament tells us there is no life in the law (Galatians 3:21). Law reveals sin. Life is found in Jesus alone.

Note the context of the Galatians passage. It is specific to redemption from the curse of the law. Through Israel, God shows us humans are inclined towards sin, and the law of God reveals this tendency by proclaiming the gold standard for living. I am so glad Jesus said yes to God's plan of redemption! When Jesus tells us to follow Him because His yoke is easy and His burden light (Matthew 11:28–30), we must understand how heavy the burden of the law was! We simply cannot live a perfect life according to God's requirements. (I know it—I've tried!)

When Jesus came, He made a new covenant between God and humans. He took all the associated punishment of the curse of the law onto Himself, hence His flogging and gruesome death. There is now a way to bypass the curse issue. Being 'born again' may be an old term, but it explains how we are translated supernaturally from the cursed lineage of Adam into the new lineage of Christ.

It's a strange thing, but since the time of Jesus, His followers have tried to pin themselves under the stone tablets.

The Blessing of Adoption

Until Jesus came, the only way for a non-Israelite (Gentile) to enter a covenant relationship with the God of Israel was for them to physically join Israel, learn their God-given laws, and keep them all. We see this example with Rahab and her family, who were rescued from Jericho and welcomed into the Israelite family.

The nations of Gentiles were not included in or held accountable to the Mosaic covenant. But this meant we also lacked a covenant relationship with God and missed out on the blessings of this relationship. The wonderful news, however, is Jesus made a way for everyone to become part of God's family. Like Abraham, faith is now the requirement. If you belong to Christ by faith, you are a spiritual descendant of Abraham. This makes you an heir according to the Promise God made to Abraham (Galatians 3:29). You *spiritually* join Israel, being grafted into the family tree (Romans 11)! Israel's purpose in history was to reveal the Messiah, who would redeem us all from the curse of sin and death. It was God's mercy to keep a remnant on the earth to guard and nurture the light of His coming. Without Israel's story, who would understand the salvation message when it arrived?

There has only ever been one plan of God; to have Himself one family centred on the Person of Jesus Christ. I particularly love this passage in The Passion Translation as it puts into plain and expressive language the beauty of our peace and unity in Jesus:

> *Our reconciling "Peace" is Jesus! He has made Jew and non-Jew one in Christ. By dying as our sacrifice, he has broken down every wall of prejudice that separated us and has now made us equal through our union with Christ.... The legal code that stood condemning every one of us has now been repealed by his command.... Two have now become one, and we live restored to God and reconciled in the body of Christ. Through his crucifixion, hatred died.* (Ephesians 2:14–16 TPT)

This is the best news! I am family. I am not distinguished by my Gentile-ness or any other characteristic, except for Jesus. Am I also able to claim some blessings of God? Yes! As an adopted child of God, I am *not* destined for curse because I have chosen to love Him and believe in His full work.

> *Israel's purpose in history was to reveal the Messiah, who would redeem us all from the curse of sin and death.*

I now receive Father's blessings as His child. The firstborn blessing has already been taken. But He is a generous Father, and there are plenty more.

While God requires us to follow His timeless and divine laws, we now have the Spirit of God supernaturally imprinting these laws on our hearts. Jesus kept every one of God's commandments. The Messiah, born of a Jewish girl from David's lineage, births God's law *in* us. This is a mystery of God!

A Ministry against Curse

Reading the Gospels, we see how Jesus defeated specific curses through His ministry. Remember, His ministry was in an Israelite context. Deuteronomy 28, our curse chapter, lists a number of diseases that would come on God's children if they abandoned His ways. Of course, disease is something that plagues all humans. Is it any surprise Jesus spent a huge part of His ministry removing disease from people? He literally broke the curse of disease from men, women, and children everywhere He went. He also removed much of the reason for disease—unclean spirits. Jesus demonstrated He was God by removing the diseases that were ultimately a result of a nation abandoning God. This was a fulfilment of God's words when He took His people from Egypt: 'I am the LORD who heals you' (Exodus 15:26).

Before Jesus was raised from the dead, He proved His Father's power over the grave. He raised more than one person to life during His ministry, revealing God has the power over death. This ultimate curse responsible for paralysing many with fear can no longer hold us captive. The antidote for the bite of Death is the Life of Jesus (John 1). So, the threat of this ultimate curse was removed when Jesus completed His work on the cross and was raised to life by the Spirit of life.

The nature of Jesus' ministry on Earth showed the Father's heart towards His people. His desire is to see us walking in the dignity of His original creation.

Curses That Land

As a believer, the curses of the law and of death are not my inheritance! Remember, I am translated to a new spiritual lineage, moving from Adam's spiritual ancestry to a new lineage flowing from Christ. But while the age of grace is upon us, curses are still flying around the earth. In the age to come, Jesus will dispel them. For now, I must be aware of God's eternal principles for life and the enemy's strategies.

One way for curses to land in a believer's life is through idolatry. Is it surprising this was the same for ancient Israel, those children of God? They continually failed to uphold God's commandment to not worship any other gods. Idolatry became a huge snare for them. It is also true that if our ancestors engaged in idolatry, the enemy has a connection with our generation unless that connection is broken. I provide the example of Daniel.

Daniel was an honourable, God-fearing man who knew God's favour in his life. Yet, Daniel still ended up in captivity with his people. He provides a heartfelt and humble example of repentance on behalf of his ancestors (Daniel 9). But he does not exclude himself from this prayer. I believe it was Holy Spirit inspired, but also because Daniel understood the baggage of generational sin. Daniel was not an idolater, but he was connected to ancestors who worshipped an array of demon gods. God still blessed Daniel and protected him! But Daniel was also in captivity because of the *issues in his lineage*. Idolatry leaves a runway-sized opening for a curse to land.

How many times do we see this issue play out in the stories of Abraham's descendants? Joshua endured the wilderness because of his people. Jeremiah's young life was far from normal because of the generations before him. Elijah was effectively homeless for over three years because of a drought curse on the land. And while repenting for his sin, King David acknowledged being brought into the world in generational sin (Psalm 51:5). This is a problem we all face! God is clear. He does not judge us for the sin of our ancestors. However, the sin of our lineage can impact our blessings here on Earth.

As a believer, the curses of the law and of death are not my inheritance!

But the excellent news is God knew His people would mess up, and He constantly provided an answer to their situation. Here is the promise He made to Solomon, revealing a way out for His people when they would inevitably find themselves under a curse:

> *When I shut up heaven and there is no rain, or command the locusts to devour the land, or send pestilence among My people, if My people who are called by My name will humble themselves, and pray and seek My face, and turn from their wicked ways,* **then I will hear from heaven, and will forgive their sin and heal their land.** *(2 Chronicles 7:13–14, emphasis mine)*

The Remedy at Calvary

The power of the work at Calvary has not lessened over the centuries. But many believers do not know how to apply the work of the cross to their lives. Sometimes we must do what Daniel did, repenting of past sins, whether ours or ancestors. At other times, we may not see our difficulties being connected to our spiritual walk, so we grin and bear it. In other words, we don't receive because we don't know to ask! But possibly the most confronting reason is the term 'believer' is not a reality. There is a lack of belief that Jesus can do anything. Jesus said when we pray in belief, we will receive whatever we ask for (Matthew 21:22). The reverse is true. Unbelief says, 'I don't expect anything to happen'. But all things are possible to those who believe (Mark 9:23).

What captivity are you living in today, passed down to you as a heritage from your ancestors? Do you see persistent patterns? Perhaps it's a condition that runs in the family? What about a genetic or health issue that keeps getting passed down? Sometimes before the healing can flow, the cause must be removed. Take it to the Curse-breaker. And trust He is the same Promise-keeper who produced an heir for Abraham and Sarah and birthed the promised Seed through a virgin named Mary. Be like the persistent widow (Luke 18) and the audacious woman who reached out to touch the edge of Jesus' garment for her healing (Luke 8). Sometimes faith feels uncomfortable and looks awkward to others. But God rewards it.

19

A God of Blessings

I recently studied ethics, and we discussed the topic of worldview. We all have a worldview made up of culture, belief, and experience that frames how we see our world. Greek philosophy and knowledge have strongly influenced the Western mindset. Greek philosophy laid the framework for secular ethics back in Aristotle's day.

When the Bible refers to Gentiles, it refers to people with a Greek mindset, as opposed to a Jewish one. A Gentile mindset may treat the Bible as a book about heaven and hell. We may base the summary of the story on the destination outcome. Further simplified into religious speech, if you're good, you go to heaven, and if you're bad, you go to hell. However, if this is your understanding of the Good Book, it is highly simplistic.

From Genesis to Revelation, we find a story of blessings and curses. There is most certainly an eternal destination, and the Bible has much to say about it. But as an earth-dweller, I need to understand what God does in my here and now.

Hope for Today

Our Lord tells us to focus on today. To live with a mindset of 'one day, it will all be over' and 'one day we will be with the Lord' may place our relationship and our reward firmly into a future not associated with our daily walk. This can be dangerous because, on the one hand, we may dissociate our behaviours with our ever after, and on the other hand, we may fret we will never make it.

I've experienced the destructive ploy of a dissociated and religious mindset, informing the uninitiated they can only 'hope' for this future 'someday.' What a joyless mental space to reside. We are children of inheritance and Hope—the capital H kind that exists now and extends to the future. The great I Am redeems our yesterday, involves Himself in our today, *and* holds our tomorrow.

We do not have a faith that pins all its hope on a far, far, away. In fact, God was extremely clear in setting up conditions for a relationship with His people that guided their daily reliance on Him. They were to rely on Him for *every* need, and He never let them down. Moses recounts the physicality of their journey in Deuteronomy 29, recalling their clothes and shoes did not wear out. It forced them to rely on God, and they needed this lesson.

God knows we need a now answer. This is why He lived *with* His people in the wilderness. They needed it, and so do we. We should rely on God for everything in the same way the Israelites did. This is part of the laid-down life of a believer. The God who lived daily with the Israelites is the same Jesus who walked daily with God's children on Earth. He is the same God that now permanently dwells with us by His Spirit. He is a personal, 'now' God, not a distant God, waiting to receive us into the pearly gates if we are good at the end of our journey. (This is an example of partial truth—and partial truth can destroy faith just as much as a lie can.)

We do not have a faith that pins all its hope on a far, far, away.

The Lord God told Moses He was taking His people to a land filled with blessings (milk and honey represent this blessing). This promise was a now word. God gave the people encouragement for today. It is not His fault they delayed the outcome! Our God desires for us to experience His blessings as we walk His earth today. Knowing He cares for us today inspires us to love Him and continue on the faith journey.

Our Now God

It is God's nature to bless His children. The first use of the word blessing is in Genesis 1 when God blessed the creatures of the sea and the birds of the air. As His children, we are called to be like Him. In this section, we'll see how God meets individuals at their point of need and within their earthly timeline. We also see how His blessing to certain individuals spilled out into a bigger plan, as it did with Abraham. I pray the following examples will inspire you to seek many more! Reading about God's blessings down to the smallest detail is a faith-building exercise. It helps us grow spiritual muscle and desire to experience His blessings for ourselves. Remember, He is the God of your today, who knows you so intricately even every hair on your head is numbered (Luke 12:7)!

Noah's Rainbow

After the flood and Noah's exit from the ark, God begins again with a blessing to 'Be fruitful and multiply…' (Genesis 6). He begins with a blessing and moves on to a covenant, promising to never again destroy the earth by flood, despite humankind's evil. The sign of this covenant is, of course, the rainbow. We may have become so accustomed to seeing rainbows we miss the point. But imagine being Noah for a moment! Wouldn't that sign of a rainbow be very reassuring to you? God is effectively telling Noah and his family, 'It's okay. I promise not to use this rain to destroy the earth again. You won't need to build another ark to save yourselves. I am a God who keeps My word'. While the sign remains in place as a covenant symbol, it had a 'now' purpose for Noah and his descendants.

Sarah's Little Lamb

From the blessing to Abraham, God also met Sarah's deep desire to be honoured as a mother:

> *I will make you a great nation; I will bless you and make your name great; and you shall be a blessing. I will bless those who bless you, and I will curse him who curses you; and in you all the families of the earth shall be blessed.* (Genesis 12:2–3)

Sarah suffered because of her inability to conceive a child, but God blessed her with a baby in her arms as an elderly woman. And this wasn't any baby. This baby would be an ancestor to the Messiah, through whom all of us on the earth would be blessed.

This is an amazing personal story, with a profound overflow to the entire world. God doesn't do small blessings!

The God Who Sees Hagar

Sarai's Egyptian maidservant Hagar was blessed to discover God's personal and attentive nature. After running away from her mistress while pregnant, the Angel of the Lord visited her by a spring of water in the wilderness (Genesis 16). Hagar is awed by the fact this God sees her; He actually sees her difficulty and personally comes to find her in the wilderness and interact with her. He also blesses her with the promise her son will birth many descendants.

The Lord tells Hagar to call her son Ishmael 'because the Lord has heard your affliction' (Genesis 16:11). In true ancient style, the encounter inspires the well's name, Beer-lahai-roi, or 'Well of the Living One Who Sees Me' (Genesis 16:14 AMP). We see similarities in the story of the woman at the well. Jesus was intentional in seeking this woman out and blessing her with the promise of living water. She, like Hagar, needed the personal encouragement of the Lord in a difficult situation.

A Mother's Blessing for Rebekah

The male relatives of the soon-to-be wife of Isaac blessed their sister and daughter with fruitfulness as a mother:

> *Our sister, may you become the mother of thousands of ten thousands; And may your descendants possess the gates of those who hate them.* (Genesis 24:60)

At first, her blessing didn't seem to work! Isaac had to ask God for healing over her womb, as she could not have children. But she became the mother of two great nations through Jacob and Esau. Rebekah is also an example of someone who was blessed through being yoked to the lineage of Promise. As Isaac's wife, she became part of Abraham's blessing, which God confirmed to her husband (Genesis 26).

Jacob's Stew

This blessing is tough to swallow because Esau despised it, and Jacob took it through deception. But the blessing still stuck! Here we see the power of a father's blessing. The sons of these ancients waited in expectation for the father's blessing. Esau, who was focused on his stomach at the time, sold his birthright (the eldest son's blessing) to Jacob for some stew (Genesis 25). Jacob dressed as Esau and deceived his blind father Isaac to receive the firstborn blessing with a bit of help from his mum. Isaac ignorantly blessed his second-born with these prophetic words:

> *Surely, the smell of my son*
> *Is like the smell of a field*
> *Which the LORD has blessed.*
> *Therefore may God give you*
> *Of the dew of heaven,*
> *Of the fatness of the earth,*
> *And plenty of grain and wine.*
> *Let peoples serve you,*
> *And nations bow down to you.*
> *Be master over your brethren,*
> *And let your mother's sons bow down to you.*
> *Cursed be everyone who curses you,*
> *And blessed be those who bless you!*
> (Genesis 27:27–29)

Now read them again, but this time realise these words came to pass! The blessing of Jacob is Israel's story. It reveals the continuation of this blessing through his lineage because it was a confirmation of the blessing God had given to his father and grandfather.

The Lion of Leah

Hidden in Leah's somewhat plain story are treasures that reveal the God Who Sees. Poor Leah. She didn't exactly have a choice in deceiving Jacob and being married off to him. I can only imagine her heartbreak the morning after the wedding. Leah became an unloved wife, but the Lord saw her situation (Genesis 29:31), and He gave her children, sons no less, to continue the lineage. For these women of old, children were a most anticipated blessing, and being unable to conceive caused much distress, as we see in the conflict between Sarai and Hagar.

Leah recognised her blessing as being from the Lord, and she named her sons accordingly. She is truly a blessed woman in Abraham's lineage, being the mother of Judah, head of the tribe of Judah—which produced the Lion of Judah. Leah, the unloved wife of Jacob, became one of the most blessed women in history because the Lord saw her and determined to bless her.

Our Father's Heart

God has a father's heart. He is the ultimate example of what a father should do and how a father should love. He also reveals how an earthly father should bless. The pattern of the firstborn blessing is present when we examine God and Israel. Israel was his firstborn. To Israel, He gave the special blessing of birthing the Messiah and presenting Him to the world through His holy people. Israel was chosen for a task no other child of God could do.

However, Father God has intentionally set up the family structure to invite many more children into His fatherly embrace. The nations are also His inheritance. He longs to be in a relationship with the people He created. Perhaps surprisingly, this includes the nation of Egypt. The nation God used to develop and form His firstborn has a place in His heart. While the judgement prophecies of Isaiah against Egypt are harsh, eventually, God will restore her.

> *In that day Israel will be one of three with Egypt and Assyria—a blessing in the midst of the land, whom the LORD of hosts shall bless, saying, "Blessed is Egypt My people, and Assyria the work of My hands, and Israel My inheritance."* (Isaiah 19:24–25)

Wow! Egypt, 'My people'? God's heart is for blessing and relationship.

An earthly father's blessing may be imperfect, but the blessing of our heavenly Father is perfect. Jesus tells us a bit of the Father's heart in the well-known 'Ask, Seek, Knock' passage (Luke 11). It is absolutely not our Father's heart to give gifts other than good ones. The punch line of the passage is, 'How much more will your heavenly Father give the Holy Spirit to those who ask Him!' (v. 13).

The ultimate gift and provision of Father God to His children is the very essence of Himself living with us. Unlike Hagar, we don't have to wait for a visit by a well. Our new covenant position means Father places a well of living water *in us*. This living water is the Spirit of Christ. His Spirit is continually with us and knows all our needs. What a blessing from our heavenly Father.

The Blessing of Ministry

As end-time saints, we are privileged to have the gifts of the Spirit at our disposal. We are blessed to participate in the ministry of the saints and usher in the kingdom of God. You see, God has not left us saved and idle on planet Earth. The call to Abraham and Moses is still the call to us. We are the body of Christ, positioned under His headship. Like Abraham, we are called to birth a spiritual nation. Like Moses, we are called to equip it. Through the ministry of the gospel, we see others join the family, and we see them become fulfilled as they step into their God-given gifts and callings and out of the world's counterfeit identity.

Arise, you evangelists, prophets, and teachers! The world needs you and every other gift and calling given by the Spirit. Under the instruction of his father-in-law, Moses selected leaders to support him in his large and exhausting task of governing the people of Israel (Exodus 18). The job was too big for one man! Pastors have their job descriptions, but it doesn't include carrying the flock on their back. It's time for pew dwelling to cease and the blessing designed to come from us as individuals to flow out.

The call to Abraham and Moses is still the call to us.

You are designed as a unique vessel of blessing! No other created being can do what you can do. Each one of us has a specific sphere of influence. Pause for a moment and consider how many lives you interact with in a day, a week, or a month. If you are feeling a tad courageous, write some of those names down and start praying about how you can bless them. There is no one-size-fits-all approach. Ask the Holy Spirit how you can best express Jesus and shine His light. He knows exactly what each person needs.

20

We Are the Mouthpiece of God

Bless those who persecute you; bless and do not curse. (Romans 12:14)

The Israelites and the ancient peoples knew curses were real. In our Western mindset, we do not have the same spiritual understanding. We tend to think these things can't happen, or they belong in fictitious books about wizards. But the ancients operated with a full understanding of the power of curses.

Balak's Failed Attempt

The story of Balak and Balaam in Numbers (22–24) gives us helpful insight into the general theme of pronouncing curses on people. When the children of Israel arrived on the plains of Moab, Balak became concerned. He knew they had destroyed the mighty Amorite kings, Sihon and Og. Moab was terrified of the large group of Israelites camped so close to them. What to do? Balak has a thought, 'I know! I will get someone to curse them!' He seeks Balaam—a known prophet.

Balaam is an interesting character. He hears from God and interacts with Him, but he is not a sold-out prophet for God. Despite the insistence of Balak and pressure from concerned princes, Balaam is unable to curse the Israelites. In fact, three times, he opens his mouth, and each time a blessing comes out instead of a curse. Balak is pretty annoyed the guy he hired to curse his enemy is pouring out blessings on them. Balaam's justification is he cannot go beyond the word of the Lord regarding these people. His fourth attempt is a major fail as far as Balak is concerned when he overtly proclaims Messiah and gives a word to Balak on the unfortunate future of Moab. Instead of curses on Israel, Moab received a curse.

The God of Israel is jealous for His children. No one would curse the people He had blessed. Balak must have been ignorant of the Promise to Abraham that God would bless people who blessed Israel and He would curse those who cursed her (Genesis 12:3). Therefore, Balak's intent to curse Israel was turned against him.

If God is a God of blessing, His covenant people should be a people of blessing. The spiritual children should reflect their Father. We are called to use our words with wisdom, cultivated from the prayer room, not from the newsroom.

The Power of the Tongue

It is important to understand how our words impact our world. Words hurled in anger, hate, or revenge can do permanent damage to a vulnerable heart and mind, particularly if they are from a family member or someone in a position of trust. Alternatively, words spoken in accordance with God's plans and purposes are powerful to bring change and heal hearts and minds. I have experienced both types of words. You probably have, too. The words of life sound different, and they produce a positive, life-changing outcome.

According to the writer of Proverbs 18, our tongue holds the power of life or death (v. 21). That is a terribly responsible position! God designed us to be His mouthpiece on the earth, just as He called Moses to be His mouthpiece in our story. As humans, we have the power to bless and curse others, but as believers, we are told only to bless. If blessings and curses both flow from the mouth of a believer, it would be like a spring producing simultaneously sweet and bitter water (James 3). James makes his point well. God designed us to release the sweet water of the Spirit. Bitter water has no refreshing qualities and will only make others sick.

We are called to use our words with wisdom, cultivated from the prayer room, not from the newsroom.

Blessing is proactive and is based in God's kingdom. It is spoken by faith and is not limited to the natural view of someone's experience. We see this in Abraham's story. Isaac, the promised son, was humanly an impossibility. When blessing others from God's kingdom perspective, we bring down the plan of God for that individual, from heaven to Earth. How do I know this? Because Jesus taught us to pray, 'Your kingdom come. Your will be done *on earth, as it is in heaven*' (Matthew 6:10). We proclaim God's purposes and His kingdom over lives. We break the words of the enemy by coming against his lies with God's truth. Blessing is not just a nice thing to do. A blessing can break the strongholds of the enemy and chase the Balaks out of our territory.

So why are blessings so powerful? When we speak with God's words through His Spirit, we speak substance—just like He did at creation. Things appeared in the physical realm that had not previously existed. We may not see peace flow through a room, but by faith, we expect it to! Like Daniel, we can learn how God may bring answers on the wings of angels, but also that blessings may take time to work themselves out in the natural. This may test our faith, but the story of Daniel should also inspire us to develop a tenacious, expectant faith when it comes to receiving an answer from the throne of God.

God seriously loves to bless. I don't believe His church has woken to the power of blessing as she should. What we have been given, we should give away. Imagine the good we can do by speaking blessing everywhere we go. Think of the change we can bring when we bless our children and loved ones, our workplaces, and our communities. Imagine the environments we can change through our words. If we truly believe the God of creation is in us, it won't be difficult to believe our speech is empowered by His word to bring life. John 1 succinctly presents Jesus as Creator, Word, and Life. These three attributes are woven together. We take on Jesus; we have access to His attributes!

Be a Multiplier

The blessing of multiplication is the opposite of lack or reduction. I see this principle in many places in Scripture, but it begins in Genesis and first comes from God's mouth. Pray multiplication over you and yours, over your life and ministry, and over the areas God has given you influence. Pray for multiplication of the seed of the gospel sown in faith, even up to one hundred times (Parable of the Sower)! Imagine having one hundred people hear about God's goodness because you sowed one seed and prayed in faith over it.

Our faith is supernatural. When we only expect a natural answer to prayer, we limit the outcome to what our rational mind can understand and cope with. That is not faith. Without big, bold faith, we cannot pray big, bold prayers. Don't leave the concept of blessing in theory land.

Words as Curses

When we bless, we come into agreement with God, and the power of our words is a weapon against the enemy. When we curse, we come into agreement with the enemy. The definition of cursing means to utter words to bring misfortune to someone. This is exactly what Barak tried to get the prophet Balaam to do to Israel. It is a fleshly form of witchcraft designed to harm or control someone. Sadly, we often curse ourselves with our careless words. Cursing comes easily until the Spirit of God has His way in our hearts. It's so easy to spit out a damaging word and impossible to take it back.

> *Beware of counterfeit seeds planted by the counterfeit sower.*

As God's mouthpieces, we must be diligent to ensure our words come from a pure vessel. When we partner with negativity, disappointments, anger, confusion, or any bad thoughts or ways of living, our pure flow of Spirit-filled words quickly becomes tainted. The person at the receiving end may receive a mixture of the sweet and bitter water James refers to. Unfortunately, bitterness taints everything! Eventually, unresolved bitter heart wounds will flow out with the Spirit's sweet words. This brings confusion when people hear two different voices coming from someone who claims to know God's voice. As God's mouthpiece, we must guard our hearts because out of our hearts flow the issues of life (Proverbs 4:23).

For a mouthpiece of God to be effective, it needs to be maintained and kept clean. This is a daily exercise! Ultimately, the devil's plan is to damage our God-given identity. Satan does *not* want us to know or believe who we really are! Encouraging people to speak the opposite of God's thoughts about us is just one of his specialties, and word curses can be highly destructive. We can partner with these words through our acceptance or fear of them. They then become the enemy's fiery arrows Paul talks about (Ephesians 6:16).

Children are particularly vulnerable to believing things about themselves that are not what God says about them. If these words are not dealt with, they form a belief system. When I became a mature adult, I finally realised many adults are big people with unhealthy childhood belief systems. In fact, this is sadly very normal. Many adults still live with the pain of negative words spoken over them as children. Words from childhood can permanently damage a fragile soul. Thankfully, Jesus is the answer.

So, what is a word curse? I've prepared some simple and common examples. You may prefer to think of them as the enemy's word versus God's word.

What if…

- your child was being told daily at school they are worthless or dumb?

- you are continually told you are ugly, fat, useless, or (insert word curse here)?

- you are told you don't have anything to offer in your church?

- your parent continually devalued you or your thoughts and emotions?

- you are a believer with recurring thoughts about yourself that bring shame or cause you to question who you are or your worth?

Of course, we know pain results from these scenarios. The last point is a direct implant by the enemy. I know this one particularly well. It is also hugely successful because you tend to think all thoughts are your own. Newsflash! They are not. Beware of counterfeit seeds planted by the counterfeit sower.

The old adage that words can never hurt us is false! They most certainly can, and they do. People take their lives over repeated word attacks, revealing the level of torment they can cause. If you are guilty of perpetrating word curses, you need to stop, repent, and address the harm done by asking the Lord to break off the harmful effects of the words spoken. You can then replace these words with a blessing over the ones you have damaged.

> *We must not open any spiritual doors to the enemy, who snoops around looking for an opportunity to partner with our false step and play a spiritual game of snakes and ladders with us.*

A child's vulnerability to attacks on their identity should martial us as parents, guardians, and loved ones to be in continual prayer for them so the enemy cannot get his word in. The stronger a faith shield is, the better it can resist the enemy's fiery darts. We form a faith shield around our children when we stand against the enemy's work and words on their behalf, deflecting the words from their fragile souls. Roman soldiers were known for their shield formation in battle, covering each other in a protective 'shell' or wall of shields. When we partner with others in prayer, our collective faith shields are joined together, and the enemy struggles to get any fiery arrows through. There is power in the two or three gathered together in prayer (Matthew 18:20).

Calling Faithful Warriors!

Pray for your children, grandchildren, and the little ones you know! Pray power prayers, not insipid ones. Get angry against Satan's taunts and insults (not people). Use your mouth to declare God's purposes over your loved ones. Pour blessing over them and use your authority in the Spirit to come against the devil's accusations and mind games. The story of Israel proclaims every time God spoke, His word *always* defeated Israel's enemy. We must learn the art of wielding the sword of the word of God!

> *So shall My word be that goes forth from My mouth; it shall not return to Me void, but it shall accomplish what I please, and it shall prosper in the thing for which I sent it.* (Isaiah 55:11)

The enemy wages war over our minds, and God's children are not immune. The very blessed and perfect Adam and Eve discovered this the hard way. It worries me many believers are in denial of a spiritual enemy. They walk around with long faces, telling themselves their defeated mind is part of the Christian burden when, in fact, the devil has deceived them too. Even the amazing and humble Moses hijacked his entry to the Promised Land because He failed to revere the word of the Lord as instructed. It is so easy to think we know better!

If I am labouring a point, bear with me. The word of God is what the enemy goes after. He hates it! Don't be a mouthpiece for the enemy through word curses, anger, or sowing seeds of doubt.

To be a faithful mouthpiece, we must not open any spiritual doors to the enemy, who snoops around looking for an opportunity to partner with our false step and play a spiritual game of snakes and ladders with us. Ensure you are not harbouring any anger, hate, bitterness, or unforgiveness towards others. Keep a short list of offences and get rid of the list before you go to sleep each night. (God does not accept our offerings when there is an offence in our hearts, which should give us a clue how He feels about this.) Partnering with offence is a sure way to pollute those sweet waters.

> *Whoever guards his mouth and tongue keeps his soul from troubles.* (Proverbs 21:23)

To end this chapter, I've crafted a daily prayer from Scripture for you to pray over yourself. Pray it in faith. You can also include your loved ones. Praying Scripture is powerful because the Lord responds to His word. With the guidance of the Spirit, you can adapt this prayer to your own situation.

Without big, bold faith, we cannot pray big, bold prayers.

A Warrior's Prayer of Protection

In the Name of Jesus (Yeshua), I apply the *helmet of salvation* to protect my mind in Christ (Messiah). I claim the *breastplate of righteousness*, which is the righteousness of Christ that allows me to stand before the throne of grace. I put on the *belt of truth* to stand against the enemy's lies and protect God's word in me. On my feet are the *shoes of the gospel of peace*, enabling me to walk in and share the peace I have found with God through Jesus.

In my hand, I take up the *shield of faith* to withstand the enemy's fiery arrows and protect the truth in my mind and heart. I pray an enlarged faith shield around me and my loved ones. I wield the *sword of the Spirit*, which is the word of God, and declare it will go out from my mouth with power, justice, love, and mercy, truthfully representing Jesus and not returning void. Over it all, I plead the blood that washes me clean and protects me.

Anoint my mouth and my heart, Lord, so my words will be anointed as a member of your priesthood. Set a guard over my mouth, so I always speak Your words and represent You faithfully. I declare I am a blessing to others because You first blessed me. Thank You for Your heavenly protection and life.

Amen[1]

21

Taking Ground

All these people earned a good reputation because of their faith, yet none of them received all that God had promised. For God had something better in mind for us, so that they would not reach perfection without us. (Hebrews 11:39–40 NLT)

In reaching the land of Promise, it would seem the hard years were behind them, but the children of Israel had much work ahead to claim victory over the land. Part of the reason for them inheriting Canaan was God's judgement on the sin of its occupants. Under Joshua's leadership, it was now time for this evil to be punished. The wilderness years had birthed and honed troops under Israel's tribe leaders, and God would use them collectively to bring about His judgement.

The Perfect Warrior
Joshua learned the art of war by being in God's presence. The warfare of Joshua is the primary purpose of Christ—to defeat the enemy and provide safety and rest for the children. We find a big Messianic clue

in Jesus' authority over demons. He cast these squatters out from the inheritors of Promise, cleansing and preparing the new Tabernacle of God in the process.

In Joshua's day, the people learned that only God's supernatural power could defeat Satan's earthly warlords, the giants. Joshua's task was to cleanse the land of its unholy inhabitants. The fact Jesus did this same spiritual work revealed Him to be God. Jesus' mission to His governmental body on Earth hasn't changed. We are called to break the enemy's power over the lives and destinies of people, freeing them so they can choose Jesus. To us, He gives the ministry of the gospel, including baptism, deliverance, healing the sick, and raising the dead. This work takes us beyond simply holding our spiritual ground. It is designed to advance His kingdom, in the manner of Joshua in the land of Promise.

And as you go, preach, saying, 'The kingdom of heaven is at hand.' Heal the sick, cleanse the lepers, raise the dead, cast out demons. Freely you have received, freely give. (Matthew 10:7–8)

What's with the Canaanites?

When God made His covenant with Abraham for the land of Canaan, He named ten people groups as inhabitants of the land (Genesis 15). Seven of these groups continue to get mentioned in the story—the Canaanites, Hittites, Amorites, Perizzites, Hivites, Jebusites, and Girgashites.

The Canaanites were the family group of Canaan, Noah's grandson. Canaan's sons gave birth to the family groups of the Jebusite, Amorite, Girgashite, Hivite, and others (Genesis 10:15–18). What happened to turn this line towards evil for generations?

After the Flood, Noah became drunk and took a nap naked (Genesis 9:20–21). Noah's son Ham dishonoured his father in this vulnerable state, which caused Noah to curse Ham's son Canaan (Genesis 9:24–27). From this time, we see the propensity in the family line towards evil. Israel's destiny is to deal with this curse. Canaan's evil proliferated until God said, 'Enough!' giving the land of Canaan into the hand of his brothers' descendants, in accordance with the prophecy of Noah.

The Amorites get quite a mention in this infamous family group. God specifically identified the sins of the Amorites when making His covenant with Abram (Genesis 15:12–16), which gives us a clue about their importance. The Egyptians depicted the Amorites on their monuments as fair-skinned and blue-eyed, with aquiline noses and pointed beards.[1] They were warlike mountaineers[2] and appeared to have been imposing, given their ancestral connection with giants.

Under Moses' leadership, the Lord took the Israelites to victory in two battles against Amorite kings. They defeated Sihon, and Og of Bashan, from the giant lineage. God used these significant victories to develop his large army in the wilderness, strengthening their courage and resolve and striking fear into the heart of their enemies (Joshua 2:9).

The Amorites were used as tools in the hand of God, the Commander of Israel's armies, honing them into warriors. We all need to build on our previous victories and successes to gain confidence for the next big thing in our lives. For Israel, this meant fighting more Amorites in their new land.

Jericho Has Fallen!

Once in Canaan, God gave the people an early victory. He did not allow them time to wonder or worry. But first, Joshua oversaw the circumcision of the Red Sea generation as a sign of covenant with their God. While the men rested in their new camp at Gilgal, the people partook in Passover, reminding them of God's deliverance from death, before they took on the Canaan warriors. How like God to orchestrate the timing of entry with His Passover. The day after Passover, heaven's manna stopped, and the people enjoyed produce from Canaan. At last, the milk and honey had arrived!

As Joshua waited in this quiet interval, the Commander of the Army of the Lord appeared to him. I'm sure he was encouraged to know supernatural reinforcements were in place!

We all need to build on our previous victories and successes to gain confidence for the next big thing in our lives.

Jericho was not won by human strength. You really can't drop thick stone walls with standard trumpet blasts. However, obedience *was* required. Six days of walking quietly around the wall once, with the priests blowing trumpets, was followed by the seventh day of walking around the wall seven times. Finally, on Joshua's command, the walking army, complete with priests and the Ark of the Covenant, gave an enormous shout while the trumpets declared victory. Without a sword drawn, the walls gave up! Down they came, surrendering the city to the men of Israel. Do we believe this story of old? Do we think it has any relevance to us today? I do. Let me tell you a slightly unusual story…

Recently, during a period of pressing in for answers about a long spiritual battle that holds no human answers, I was reminded of the wall of Jericho. This wall was impassable, but its removal did not require physical strength. It only required obedience. I had been walking around our city's lake when the idea came to me. Over the course of that day, I walked around it seven times before loudly announcing Jesus to my wall. My walk had nothing to do with the city or the lake. It had to do with me pressing into God's promises and making a prophetic declaration against the enemy's wall. This was between God and me.

By faith, I have determined to believe that in the supernatural arena beyond my physical senses, God is working on my behalf—just like he did for Daniel. The word of God tells me we do not fight against flesh and blood. We fight the war that rages supernaturally (Ephesians 6). (Since I wrote this, the supernatural shaking has begun in earnest!)

The Sin of Achan

The walls of Jericho may have fallen as easily as a sandcastle, but Joshua was not prepared for the wall of despair that slammed him next. After a knock-out victory, a simple battle turned into a nightmare failure. Joshua was distraught. He sought the Lord as he lay before the ark, questioning why God would allow this defeat.

The Lord finally spoke, somewhat curtly, telling Joshua an Israelite had defiled the camp by taking things from Jericho and bringing curses with them. On multiple occasions, God had told the Israelites what would happen if they ignored His instruction and entertained other gods. He had also given the people explicit instruction to not take anything 'accursed' from Jericho, or they would cause the camp of Israel to be cursed and bring trouble to it (Joshua 6:18). Could the Lord have been clearer? No. Could He ignore this transgression, fresh into Promise? He could not. A little leaven spreads through the whole dough.

This terrible sin resulted in Achan's death, along with his family (Joshua 7). Once the sin was dealt with, victory was assured. This Scripture passage is a tough read, but it should also bring an understanding of how powerful Jesus' sacrifice is. Achan had to die for his sin because the penalty for his disobedience under the law was death. Note his sin destroyed his entire family line. If Achan lived today, he could have repented and allowed the ongoing cleansing of the blood of Jesus to restore him and his family. THAT is the difference Jesus makes.

The Risk of Assumption

Even in obedience and promise, we need to be wary of deception, including overconfidence in our ability to understand the spiritual realities around us. Of all the victories Joshua could claim in the land of Promise, Gibeon was not one of them (Joshua 9).

It seems the Gibeonites were a bit smarter than the rest of the inhabitants of Canaan. They were practical and proactive. Gibeon was considered a mighty house amongst their neighbours. Instead of waiting for their demise at the hand of this new group of inhabitants, they hatched a clever plan. As neighbours of the newly arrived Israelites, the Gibeonites sent a delegation to the leaders of Israel. Dressed in rags with carefully staged mouldy provisions, this band of diplomats approached Gilgal, where Joshua and his men camped.

The men of Israel were definitely wary of them. However, after speaking with the convincing Gibeonite actors and assessing their dry, mouldy bread and torn wineskins, the men of Israel decided they must be the long-distance travellers they proclaimed to be. Their words matched their appearance. The key issue in this passage is Joshua and his leaders did not ask the Lord about the situation (Joshua 9:14). They knew not to make peace with the neighbours, but assumed after an assessment by their natural ear and eye these men were telling the truth. Joshua's men assessed the situation at face value only. It wasn't long before the Gibeonites were found out, but it was too late for the rulers of Israel to do anything. They had already made a covenant of peace with them in the name of the God of Israel. There was no way they could break it.

The men of Israel were not pleased with this news, but they had to accept it. All they could do now was to subdue the Gibeonites and bring them into forced labour. So Joshua subjected them to the roles of woodcutters and water carriers for the house of God. The Gibeonites accepted this, preferring to live in subjugation than die by Israel's sword. Although not ideal, apparently, this arrangement worked out reasonably well, as you don't hear about the Gibeonites until much later when Saul broke the covenant with them, and there were consequences for Israel (2 Samuel 21). At this point in Israel's history, we discover the Gibeonites were a remnant of the Amorites! Somehow, this little city full of Amorites snuck past the guard.

We need wisdom and discernment daily, not forgetting our understanding is limited and we are prone to deceiving ourselves.

We must be ready for deception. See how easy it is to be deceived, especially if we only use our natural senses? Jesus told His disciples that in the end times, our world will be so bad even the true followers of God would be in danger of being deceived (Matthew 24:24).

I don't know about you, but I find these words of Jesus confronting and concerning. But God has provided His special gift of discernment to protect us from deception.

Safety in Discernment

We sorely need the gift of discernment in the house of God. Discernment enables us to pick the difference between good and evil spirits (1 Corinthians 12:10). It is a key gift of protection. Collecting evidence from two or three witnesses is a principle of God. And He has provided us with two powerful witnesses—a book of wisdom and instruction (the Bible) and His Spirit. Reading God's word helps us learn what deception looks like. Christ's Spirit in us witnesses to the written word and brings revelation and understanding. Together, the two protect us against the enemy's counterfeits and twisting of God's words, which is what tripped Eve up.

Only the Spirit brings the gift of discernment (1 Corinthians 12). It is not a natural gift, as we see in Israel's interaction with the Gibeonites. Can you think of times you've been surprised by a turn of events because you didn't discern the spiritual cues? How did that make you feel?

We need wisdom and discernment daily, not forgetting our understanding is limited, and we are prone to deceive ourselves. As we get closer to the return of Jesus, it could literally be a matter of life or death.

Also, beware of misplaced compassion. Yes, there is such a thing! Compassion is a beautiful gift from God. But false mercy can sometimes be our downfall, as we second guess our Lord's commands and think His judgements harsh. God warned the people of this before they entered Promise, telling them not to show mercy on the list of nations He explicitly told them to destroy. God had already shown them mercy by allowing them *centuries* to repent of their wicked ways. Instead, they continued to worship other gods and sacrifice their children to them.

God knows what will happen if we listen to our hearts over His word. He is a perfect God of justice. Without justice, there can be no genuine love because perfect love demands justice. False mercy often views one party's needs over the needs of others. This is seen in Solomon's downfall. He thought his wives should be able to worship the gods of their lands. The renowned man of wisdom lost his way because he gave his heart to his wives and their gods, turning away from his God and his strong duty towards Israel.

Discernment is a much-needed spiritual essence in our lives. Let the sobering story of Solomon and the subsequent decline of Israel teach us we can give our promise away to a tugging of the heartstrings.

God knows what will happen if we listen to our hearts over His word.

Establishing Promise

The judgement on Canaan was one part of God's plan. Establishing His children in their own special land was the second part, just as He promised Abraham all those years ago. The establishment of Promise meant making a home in Canaan. It involved putting down roots, worshipping God according to His many feasts (He is a God of joy and celebration!), and beginning a new life that looked much different from a camp in the wilderness. Stone, timber, and mortar provided a firmer foundation than tent pegs in the sand.

This was a process, not an immediate reality. God told the people how He would practically support them in taking their land of Promise (Exodus 23). One of His provisions was to drive out the enemy tribes in smaller batches. God further explains He would not drive out the enemy in one year because the land would become desolate, and the wild animals would become too numerous for the people to manage (23:29). There is a process of taking our ground. Often, we want to see God drive out the enemy immediately! But, as I am learning through personal experience, we may not easily establish ourselves in our new space and manage the wide expanses given to us. We need to multiply first…

While God is not bound by time, we are. Sometimes we need time to develop new spiritual muscles and fresh ways of thinking. We may be healed or delivered from an addiction or a sin that requires us to take our time in developing new habits to keep us healed and healthy. Healing can happen in an instant, but habits take longer to form. One way God helped Israel develop good spiritual habits was to provide actual calendar dates, times, and places for sacrifice, feasting, and worship. Spiritual habits don't keep us out of trouble by themselves, but some act as big signposts to remind us of the good God we serve. They can keep us encouraged and focused on our journey.

What are your spiritual habits to help establish you in your territory?

22

Fighting Giants

Jack and the Beanstalk captured imaginations with its bloodthirsty giant from another realm. Jack was the unfortunate trespasser. There are giants in myths across the globe, entertaining us with stories of heroism. Hercules is an easy favourite when it comes to demigods with superhuman strength. Like many myths and legends, these stories were born from an element of truth.

An Unholy Alliance

Not all the people of Canaan were giants, but the giants are important to our story. Key people groups are linked with giants, including the Amorites (Amos 2:9) and the Anakim and Rephaites (Deuteronomy 2). The last Rephaite, King Og of Bashan, was killed by the Israelites during Moses' time (Deuteronomy 3:11). Philistines had connections with the giants as well, which is evident in the story of Goliath of Gath.

I do not intend to do a comprehensive giant study, but we have to at least acknowledge the unholy alliance between the sons of God and the daughters of man, which caused a hybrid people group known as Nephilim (Genesis 6).

From the Nephilim came subsequent generations of giants. Spawning Nephilim was not God's doing but the will of creatures committed to evil. In so doing, they mocked His creation and its natural order.

We associate giants with 'fame' and 'might' only in the sense of physical achievement. They did not impress a holy God. In fact, after their arrival, violence filled the earth. To better understand why a holy God destroyed His earth and its inhabitants with a flood, we should understand the level of evil caused by this unholy alliance:

> *The [population of the] earth was corrupt [absolutely depraved—spiritually and morally putrid] in God's sight, and the land was filled with violence [desecration, infringement, outrage, assault, and lust for power]. God looked on the earth and saw how debased and degenerate it was, for all humanity had corrupted their way on the earth and lost their true direction.* (Genesis 6:11–12 AMP)

Noah was righteous. But somewhere in the family gene pool, there was corrupted DNA because we know giants continued post Flood. The lineage of Ham, who produced Canaan, fits the profile of Scripture regarding the need for another clean-out.

You don't fight giants in your own power. Fighting giants requires supernatural strength. Moses tells the people:

> *For if you carefully keep all these commandments which I command you to do—to love the Lord your God, to walk in all His ways, and to hold fast to Him—then the Lord will drive out all these nations from before you, and you will dispossess greater and mightier nations than yourselves.* (Deuteronomy 11:22–23)

They would need God's help!

With the battle of Jericho now under their belt and a history of defeating Amorites, the land feared Israel. Five Amorite kings aggressively joined forces against the Gibeonites for making peace with these warlike people who had arrived on their turf. This worked out just fine for Joshua because instead of fighting five separate battles with five kings, Joshua and his men went to the aid of Gibeon and made a surprise attack.

The Lord threw the enemy armies into a panic (Joshua 10). Israel's army took them out, but God didn't stand by watching. He threw down large hailstones from heaven, which killed more enemy men than the swords of Israel. Wow! Just like the supernatural removal of chariot wheels on the Red Sea floor, the God of Israel fought with Israel, this time using weapons of fear and hailstones. There was more… Joshua bravely asked the Lord for a miracle, decreeing the sun to stand still while Israel took revenge on their enemies. And it did. Even creation was on the side of Israel.

You don't fight giants in your own power.

This victory, including conquest of all the kings' cities and the city of Makkedah, would have given the Israelites much confidence in their God and their ability to take victory over Canaan. Finally, after a forty-year pause, things were happening!

An Incomplete Conquest

Many more battles would come until the land was blessed with peace. Joshua and his army were a powerful force to be reckoned with, and the enemy didn't stand a chance as long as God was fighting for them. Joshua rid Canaan of thirty-one kings before he had any rest. This valiant warrior provides another prophetic picture of Jesus, who ultimately disarmed the enemy (Colossians 2:15) and provided a way for all children of Promise.

Perhaps it was easier to take the ground than to hold it. We arrive at the book of Judges and read in the opening chapter the tribes did not destroy all the Canaanite inhabitants. Instead, they put some of them under forced labour. But the remaining Amorites chased Dan into the mountains, and a few more gave the house of Joseph a hard time until the people increased in number and subjected them. Note 'subjected'—they did not destroy them as commanded to.

Don't we become complacent when we are tired or when life is good and peaceful?

The Philistines also proved to be a difficult group to budge. The Anakim (giants) were largely cleaned out by Joshua but remained in Gaza, Gath, and Ashdod. Later, the great King David would wage a long war against the Philistines. These Philistines are a distinct thorn in his flesh during his lifetime. It was left to David to kill the sons of the giant of Gath, including Goliath, likely descendants of the Anakim.

The Israelites were called repeatedly to destroy the Canaanites, Hittites, Amorites, Perizzites, Hivites, Jebusites, and Girgashites. Before his death, Joshua rallied the people and exhorted them not to compromise with the Canaanites, or God would no longer drive the nations out for them (Joshua 23). Instead, we have difficult-to-budge Jebusites sharing the inheritance with Benjamin and a general compromise of God's instruction.

In time, the Angel of the Lord arrived and delivered a sobering message to the children of Israel. They hadn't done their duty:

*I led you up from Egypt and brought you to the land of which I swore to your fathers; and I said, "I will never break My covenant with you. And you shall make no covenant with the inhabitants of this land; you shall tear down their altars." But you have not obeyed My voice. Why have you done this? Therefore, I also said, "**I will not drive them out before you;** but they shall be thorns in your side, and their gods shall be a snare to you."* (Judges 2:1–3, emphasis mine)

Suddenly, the One who fought for Israel drew a line in the sand of time. He had warned them repeatedly. He had encouraged, and He had provided strength and victory. The people had fought hard and long, but they stopped too soon.

Tragically, but unsurprisingly, the Canaanites soon became a snare to the Israelites, just as God said would happen. After all their wanderings, failures, punishments, and witness to the miracles of God, you would think they may have listened to His warning about leaving the enemy in the land. Are we any different? Don't we become complacent when we are tired or when life is good and peaceful? The word of the Lord in times of trouble may powerfully speak to us and drive us to act, but in times of fatigue or bounty, this same word can appear to lose its urgency or relevance to us. In moments like these, the enemy of our souls will whisper in our ear, 'Did God really say that?'

The sin of the people in not completing the work doesn't appear to be that big. We may wonder why God was so harsh... until we keep reading the story.

After the death of Joshua and the men of war, a new generation grew up. *They* did not know the Lord or the power of His miraculous work (Judges 2:10).

Then the children of Israel did evil in the sight of the Lord, and served the Baals; and they forsook the Lord God of their fathers, who had brought them out of the land of Egypt... (Judges 2:11–12)

Since that time, the land of Promise has experienced conflict or been ruled by other nations. Sadly, Father God, who established a plan for peace and fulfilment in a land to call their own, had to watch His kids do their own thing. This resulted in painful consequences that ricocheted through history and still exist today. When I read this story, I am often shocked by how quickly the next generation turned to idolatry—until I reflect on life in our time. The story of Israel warns us today with no less urgency to listen to God's voice for our own good and to intentionally teach the next generation in the knowledge of God.

A Lesson from David

I think David provides the best practical lesson on how to fight a giant. Goliath of Gath was physically intimidating. When we face off with a powerful enemy in our lives, we often feel intimidated. It could be overt or subtle. Either way, the enemy's style is to attempt to dominate and subdue us. We might feel we no longer have a voice. Perhaps our voice has been silenced, not because we said something wrong, but because the enemy did not want the sound of the Spirit coming from our mouths.

Maybe we are sick because the enemy is using sickness to prevent us from taking our piece of promise and inheritance on this earth. It is difficult to fight the enemy when we feel sick or are in pain. We cannot live in harmony with spiritual giants. Eventually, they will take our blessing and leave us without our inheritance.

The giants we face may have names such as Fear, Apathy, Comparison, Rejection, Double-mindedness, Confusion, and many others. Many people can't seem to get free from the strongholds of the mind. No amount of counselling or personal development can permanently change their mental state. That's because these mental states all have a spiritual 'big guy' pulling the strings.

Perhaps our voice has been silenced, not because we said something wrong, but because the enemy did not want the sound of the Spirit coming from our mouths.

Where a giant has taken ground somewhere in our life, we must take it back. We absolutely cannot share territory deeded to us by God! The only way we can gain victory is to destroy the spiritual giant in our life, exactly in the pattern of Israel. And, just like Israel, we may need a little help from some friends.

The Israelites' story reveals the sad reality of not completing a spiritual clean-out. It really is exhausting fighting a giant! Physically superior, the giant has an advantage. But we need to have the eyes of David, who didn't see a giant, but a taunting, evil creature mocking his God and his people. David saw the spiritual significance. He saw the fear and cowering of Israel's army. He saw the giant as a creature to be brought into subjection to the God who gave Israel her inheritance. David saw the battle of god against God. He knew this enemy had power behind it. But he could see the smallness of the enemy's power by comparison with the power of God.

David had won battles against large creatures before. The young shepherd boy had won out against a bear and a lion. In the fields, he learned about the power of his God over creatures. He trusted his God to deliver him. And frankly, David was offended on behalf of his God and royally ticked off!

Understanding the fight is not ours but God's is important. David won because he put his faith in the God who fought Israel's battles against giants centuries earlier. He also understood what the giant represented. This was the seed of a counterfeit god against the seed of the Most High God. David's battle with Goliath is also an image of the subsequent battle between Jesus and Satan. The spirit within Goliath was weak, full of puffery and taunts. The Spirit within David was strong and easily overcame the enemy. When the stone hit, it hit the place of knowledge. Even the stone had more going for it than this guy! Physically superior, this giant had no sense of spiritual direction. He was full of vain imaginations that tried to set themselves up against the knowledge of God.

When David took off his head (as he vowed he would), we also see a spiritual principle. Once the giant (spiritual strongman) has been taken down, you can do the spring cleaning. The rest of the Philistines saw their leader topple and fled. No substance there! The children of

Israel then plundered the enemy's camp. There's a song about going into the enemy's camp and taking back what he stole from us. It's time we took back territory defiled by a giant in our lives. It's time to demand back what that giant has stolen.

Our Giant Slayer

Jesus' victory was complete and resounding, humiliating the enemy and disarming him of the power he held; the power of death. The enemy likes for us to fear death. Once fear is removed, his power shrinks. We can walk in victory over giants because Jesus has secured our victory! He defeated (past tense) all our giants when He defeated death, the biggest giant of all. Why then do we struggle so much against them? It's largely a battle of the mind. The enemy taunts, lies, and brings fear. Once we engage with the enemy, believing the taunts, threats, and false words over our lives, we become defeated in that area (and this poisons other areas of our life).

Why do we often struggle to walk in victory? Why do we often see giants stomping across our promise? It's one thing to be saved; it is really quite another to experience everything Jesus provided for us through His death and resurrection. We have to *take* the full gift He has given, open it, study it, and use it. Going to church doesn't secure victory. Reading your Bible twice a day doesn't secure victory (although it helps!). You secure victory by actioning the work of Jesus. Like Moses, you don't stand on the shore of the Red Sea and wait, reading the Scriptures. You pick up your stick (authority of Jesus), and you wave it at the obstacle standing in your way. Many shrug their shoulders at the sea and drop their heads in defeat, saying, 'It must be God's will'. No. It's God's will that we take up the authority Jesus gave us. Have you taken up your rod of authority lately?

The children of Israel had to fight their way into Canaan to take the things God had declared theirs. He made the declaration, but it required the children as an army force to plunder the enemy and possess it. Sometimes we must be earnest, even aggressive, in our pursuit of kingdom things. If we are not aggressive in taking our inherited territory, there are plenty of spiritual Canaanites ready to shove us off our own Promised Land.

We can walk in victory over giants because Jesus has secured our victory!

Jesus' followers are a peculiar tribe! We are both priesthood and army. We cannot be priests without punch. Our ministry is to people, and our mission is to take back enemy ground. In fact, there is an unusual passage in Matthew (11:12) stating the violent take the kingdom of heaven by force (Matthew 11:12). If we are not aggressive in pursuing our promise, the giants will aggressively take it from us! But, we do not fight against people. Remember, we fight against principalities, powers, and rulers in the spiritual realm (Ephesians 6:12). Our aggression is towards the devil and his giant spawn!

23

Walking in Inheritance

Do not forget the Lord when the going is good and you live in peace and plenty. (Deuteronomy 8 summary)

It is one thing to take ground with the power of God. It is quite another to hold ground. The children of Israel, now settled into the land of their inheritance, were told in no uncertain terms how this worked. If they obeyed—they stayed. As soon as they disobeyed, the repercussions would reverberate across the entire nation. Sometimes the punishments under the old covenant may seem harsh for the sins committed against God's laws. But God teaches us how sin spreads and ends up defiling the whole camp. Sadly, this continually happened to Israel.

Learning from Israel

God held His judgement back for a time, but finally, the Babylonian captivity occurred, just as God said would happen if they chose disobedience. But before this happened, the people lost God's protection and the blessings He had poured onto them. It was His mercy to give the Israelites such an obvious 'heads up' when they strayed. But they didn't seem to connect the dots. Their stubborn disobedience brought destruction to the nation.

When we see the blessings leave, we should recognise the sign of the times—literally. When blessings leave, it's a warning. It is time to turn back to God's word and governance in our lives. We hold our hard-won ground (and our blessings) when we honour God's word and apply it to our lives. Holy living is the result of applying God's word in awe and reverence.

Holiness—Still a Thing

Holiness may not be a current trending topic, even in Christian circles. But it's the foundation of the covenant with God. It stands out in the Israelites' story as the condition for entering the Lord's presence. The requirement for holiness to enter God's presence has not changed. Jesus purchased our right standing with God at the highest price possible. Holiness must be important if it costs that much to bring into our lives!

Christians sometimes say, 'Well, we are not under the law!' While the words are technically correct, often the understanding is not! We now have a different Tutor in the Holy Spirit (John 14). But it's the same God and the same requirements for holiness. God has not suddenly mellowed across the ages, becoming a benevolent grandfather who dotes on His children and turns a blind eye to their sins with a wink and a smile. No! The God of Israel is the God of Jesus who required His own Son to walk out perfect righteousness and die a grisly death because of this awful thing called sin. God says He is the same, yesterday, today, and forever, so how do we reconcile not being under the law with His requirement for holiness?

Well then, since God's grace has set us free from the law, does that mean we can go on sinning? Of course not! Don't you realize that you become the slave of whatever you choose to obey? You can be a slave to sin, which leads to death, or you can choose to obey God, which leads to righteous living. (Romans 6:15–16 NLT)

When I wake in the morning, I don't think to myself, 'Oh dear… what was commandment number sixty-four?' The Holy Spirit (the Spirit of Jesus) witnesses the Word and divine law of God to my mind and spirit. Not only that, but He also empowers me to obey God's commandments, now written on my heart (Jeremiah 31:33). I know what the word says when I read my Bible and when I listen to His still, small voice. I have been baptised into Jesus, and the Word lives in me by His Spirit. His breastplate of righteousness covers my righteousness (which amounts to zero in God's kingdom!).

With opened spiritual eyes and soft, receptive hearts, our works flow from love and gratefulness in God's provision.

Just like the Israelites, we don't have any capacity to walk out a life of righteousness by ourselves. When we accept the work of Jesus by faith, we are *credited* with His righteousness, just like Abraham was when he believed God (Romans 4). Remember, we are children of Abraham, not Moses, when we believe by faith in the Son of God.

Heart of the Law

Jesus proclaimed that until heaven and earth pass away (I'm pretty sure that hasn't happened yet?), not the smallest part of a letter of a word will be removed from the law of God (Matthew 5:18). God's righteous requirements have not changed since He wrote the stone tablets (Romans 7:12). In fact, Jesus upped the ante on holiness! He added the element of the heart, teaching His followers that sin begins in this hidden place. Jesus knew our heart is the source of our life and it is known to deceive us (Jeremiah 17:9).

Keep your heart with all diligence, for out of it spring the issues of life. (Proverbs 4:23)

With the Spirit's power, we see God's *heart* in His commandments, *not* the prescriptive letter of the law. But we also understand God determines what is right and wrong. Remember, we take the Lamb whole, and that includes the provision and conditions. But we also have the Spirit's power to enable us to walk out the righteousness of Jesus. This is the amazing grace of God!

The Spirit breathes on the word of God and brings revelation that births relationship. We see the Father's heart, and because of the power of Jesus' sacrifice, we willingly yield ourselves from a position of love—not guilt, obligation, or fear. We trust Father desires the best for us, and we believe He will come through on His word and promises.

When we look at God's word as a set of rules, we miss His heart, and we are in danger of trying to save ourselves through our works. With opened spiritual eyes and soft, receptive hearts, our works flow from love and gratefulness in God's provision. Religion is destroyed.

Jesus said the whole of the law and the words of God's prophets hang on loving God, and loving others (Matthew 22:37–40). These are the greatest commandments and reveal the heart of God's law.

Keeping the Faith

To walk in inheritance is to continue walking by faith, and this requires obedience (another non-trending word). It is obvious from the story of Israel obedience wasn't their greatest strength. It is equally obvious this decision cost them and future generations dearly.

Sadly, King Solomon's story reveals how easily a wise man of God can succumb to the slippery slope of compromise of the heart. Clearly, it was not God's wisdom he consulted when he allowed his many wives to worship false gods and bring back idolatry to Israel. He consulted his heart. As a result, the hard-won ground of his father David was lost.

Our choices can and do affect our calling and destiny.

Faith is one of those spiritual muscles we must exercise. Paul urges us to celebrate the difficult times (who is this guy?!). But he knows something about faith. We don't learn perseverance in cushy times; we learn it through times of pain, doubt, frustration, and battle. The act of pushing through is what produces character. And character births hope. We need all the hope we can get in these challenging times, don't we? Our hope is not 'I hope it will all work out,' it's the hope that doesn't disappoint because of what God has done. The Spirit testifies to our hearts, 'It is well with your soul.'

> *And not only this, but we also celebrate in our tribulations, knowing that tribulation brings about perseverance; and perseverance, proven character; and proven character, hope;*

and hope does not disappoint, because the love of God has been poured out within our hears through the Holy Spirit who was given to us. (Romans 5:3–5 NASB)

Honouring His House

I will live in them and walk among them. I will be their God, and they will be my people. (2 Corinthians 6:16 NLT)

As believers, we are bonded to Christ, becoming one with Him in spirit. The body of Christ becomes the Tabernacle of the living God—the place on Earth where the Spirit of God dwells. If God had requirements for holiness for Him to live amongst the people who worshipped in a physical Tabernacle, how much more should the followers of Jesus be holy? We are the ones walking around with the Spirit of God *in us*; this privilege was purchased at immense cost. God's Tabernacle is a holy place. This is one reason God has boundaries for sexual union:

Run from sexual sin! No other sin so clearly affects the body as this one does. For sexual immorality is a sin against your own body. Don't you realize that your body is the temple of the Holy Spirit, who lives in you and was given to you by God? You do not belong to yourself, for God bought you with a high price. So you must honor God with your body. (1Corinthians 6:18–20 NLT)

God is not out to spoil our fun. Behind the scenes in the spiritual arena, we are often oblivious to the damage we do to ourselves when we don't listen to God. Our choices can and do affect our calling and destiny. As our Father, God also desires to protect us from harm.

Living in Covenant

Covenant is something the enemy goes after. He recognises the power of such an agreement and promotes many counterfeit options. The strategy of tempting us to sin is aimed at the heart of covenant. If he can get us to break our covenant with God, he gets a major win. While Jesus says He will never leave us or forsake us, it's possible for us to run away from the redemptive power of our relationship with Him. After all, God has given people free will. Like a marriage covenant, God's covenant relies on love, trust, and fidelity. We will be safe when we remain under the protection of the Father's covenant.

Run to the Father, not away from Him! This is really important when we mess up and sin. The faster we can turn around and run back to Father, the faster we are restored into relationship. His arms are always open and there is endless forgiveness available in His covenant. The guilt of religion keeps you away from Father because it exclaims loudly you're not good enough to approach Him. Of course, we are not good enough, but that is the whole point! Jesus is. Don't waste a single hour in worry and guilt. Come running with an open heart, confessing your sins and receiving the blessing of *immediate* forgiveness, the type that forgets you ever did anything wrong. I only wish I had learned this lesson earlier in my life instead of hiding in shame.

While covenant with God means adhering to His conditions—that's where the blessing is also found!

The glorious news of the new covenant is its limitless grace. We are always invited back into the warm and willing embrace of Father. We are His children, and He delights in seeing us come home! The blood of Jesus remains in place at the mercy seat to cover our sins and provide for healing from our mistakes. The work of Jesus also removes guilt, which the law could never do (Hebrews 10). This covenant provides for our frail humanity in a way the old covenant never could.

Worship and Praise

Worship in the Tabernacle of the new covenant still requires an offering. Instead of the offerings of animals, unleavened cakes, and the fruit of grapes, we bring *ourselves* before a holy God.

> *Therefore **I urge you**, brothers and sisters, by the mercies of God, **to present your bodies** [dedicating all of yourselves, set apart] **as a living sacrifice, holy and well-pleasing to God**, which is your rational (logical, intelligent) act of worship. And do not be conformed to this world [any longer with its superficial values and customs], but be transformed and progressively changed [as you mature spiritually] by the renewing of your mind [focusing on godly values and ethical attitudes], so that you may prove [for yourselves] what the will of God is, that which is good and acceptable and perfect [in His plan and purpose for you].* (Romans 12:1–2 AMP, emphasis mine)

Our true worship is our yielded-ness. Worship is not a Sunday attitude or a song. Satan continues to vie for our worship. His words through media, song, and platforms of authority call to our hearts and minds brazenly expectant of our allegiance. The final battle of the enemy is one of worship. A believer with one foot in the world is unlikely to survive the fight over his soul, and this saddens me greatly. For a flicker of self-gratification, you can hand over your inheritance. You see, the enemy of God knows how to trade. But he trades in deception.

Woman thought she was getting the knowledge of good and evil when she ate the tasty fruit, but the devil's bait-and-switch tactic landed her in a world of hurt. When you are tempted by the world's enticements, ask yourself what you are really trading. It might be your family, your children, your hopes and dreams, or your inheritance. It could even be your salvation if you bow in worship.

> *Worship is not a Sunday attitude or a song.*

For the believer in Jesus, 'living sacrifice' means dying to self. This includes laying down our ideas and opinions on what God says. He has given us intelligence, but we should use it with wisdom and apply it with humility to avoid an intellectual idol rising in our hearts.

Along with worship, praise is a weapon of warfare! The devil hates it when we praise God. He'd much prefer us to complain like the Israelites when things don't go our way. Praise is the weapon that shuts the enemy up and causes him to shake his head in surprise and dismay, 'Why do they praise Him when I'm trying so hard to mess up their lives and make them miserable?' We praise God because He is worthy, but we praise Him because it's good for us. A garment of praise covers us and protects us from a spirit of heaviness (Isaiah 61:3). The Israelites succumbed to this spirit of despair in the wilderness with serious consequences. Lack of praise is an opportunity for the devil to get a foothold in your life.

Praise keeps us from complaining. It's very difficult to whine when you have praise coming out of your mouth! Praise literally shifts the atmosphere around you and dispels negative thoughts. The enemy cannot stand it! But, as Paul and Silas discovered, the enemy's chains are ineffective against praise (Acts 16). God's weapons for us today are unusual, but they are designed to fight a spiritual battle on the battleground of our minds and hearts. It will be a struggle at times to force praise out of your mouth, but it will be worth the minor discomfort when you realise the enemy has fled the battleground!

When Life Is Good

When life is good and the going is easy, we must be extra vigilant. Israel found herself at the greatest risk when she was living in peace and plenty. In these times, we are often lulled into a sleepy spiritual state, where the enemy's subtle whispers become our thoughts. Suddenly, we get a bit slack with our fellowship and prayer life. We convince ourselves we're just tired, or it's only for a season, but the truth is, we quickly lose our good spiritual habits and our taste for them. Entertainment numbs us as we enter alternate realities to forget about the day's inconveniences. The risk of becoming lukewarm is real!

For a flicker of self-gratification, you can hand over your inheritance.

A good soldier prepares for future battles in the downtime. You can't go to sleep during peacetime and wake up as an experienced warrior when the battle cry sounds. Good times are hard for us, but they are times to live in the blessings of God and remember where they come from. These are the times to teach our children and prepare them for the future.

Do not forget the Lord when the going is good.

24

Our Final Promise

Come to Me, all you who labor and are heavy laden, and I will give you rest. Take My yoke upon you and learn from Me, for I am gentle and lowly in heart, and you will find rest for your souls. For My yoke is easy and My burden is light. (Matthew 11:28–30)

Early in our story, the Israelites found themselves bound by the king of Egypt under the yoke of cruel slave masters. These words of Jesus in Matthew now come alive! He is the prison breaker who sets the captives free. And under His protective arm, we find safety and rest from our burdens and pain. Unlike the prideful Egyptian rulers of the day, Jesus is gentle, patient, and humble. He walks beside us as a friend.

Entering His Rest

Psalm 91 explains what we can expect when we faithfully hold the ground God has given us. When we live in the presence of Almighty God in a relationship, we remain in His shelter. He protects us, and we become warriors, stepping on the heads of the cobra and the lion (the enemy).

The promise:

He will cover you with his feathers. He will shelter you with his wings. His faithful promises are your amour and protection. (Psalm 91:4 NLT)

The condition:

If you make the Lord your refuge, if you make the Most High your shelter, no evil will conquer you; no plague will come near your home. (Psalm 91:9–10 NLT, emphasis mine)

We may overlook the scriptural principle of rest in our busy servant lives, but we can *only* do the Lord's work from a place of rest. When we understand Jesus conquered the fleshly pursuit of righteousness—our work, we understand He calls us to operate from a place of rest in Him, as Lord of the Sabbath. We rest in *His* work. We give our spiritual strivings away, and we celebrate the reality of receiving a perfect grade for an exam we did not even sit.

We hold our ground best when we are walking in peace and in His rest. We lose ground when we leave His place of rest and strive all over again. Imagine what would have happened if David battled Goliath out of fear? The whole battleground and outcome would have shifted. Today, here on Earth, we can abide in a realm of God's shelter and rest. This is the encouragement of Psalm 91.

The story of the Israelites does not end in Canaan. There is a grander, more permanent, and infinitely better place prepared for the faithful children of God from all generations. It is a permanent place of rest from our earthly pursuits:

> *Now if Joshua had succeeded in giving them this rest, God would not have spoken about another day of rest still to come. So there is a special rest still waiting for the people of God. For all who have entered into God's rest have rested from their labors, just as God did after creating the world. So let us do our best to enter that rest. But if we disobey God, as the people of Israel did, we will fall.* (Hebrews 4:8–11 NLT)

Again in this passage, we see the promise plus the condition. Obedience ultimately brings rest. We attain our final physical and spiritual resting place with Jesus, dependent upon how we treat the word of God today. Where we mess up—He is faithful to forgive us. Don't confuse holiness with perfection! God is perfect. We are a work in progress. It's not about our perfection. It's about our obedience. Our obedience will do a work in us that births holiness in our lives.

Trying to be 'good' will go wrong very quickly. We cannot attain the legal perfection of the law. That is why we need Jesus. Hold on to His word, and do what He says. Don't test Him as Israel did. Trust Him. Obedience is really that complex—and that simple. If you mess up, He is there to rescue you. His blood is the ever-present spiritual cleanser you need.

Don't confuse holiness with perfection!

There is a final promise yet to come—the final crossing over, where we enter permanent rest. The rewards will be huge! Let's not forget the reality of storing up treasures for the forever event in our future—treasures with a spiritual currency far surpassing the world's treasure stores. You cannot take your worldly treasures to your eternal destination, so don't spend your time and effort storing perishables. They hold no kingdom value.

At the end, there is a final Sabbath rest for the faithful. This rest is not like resting after a hard day's work. This rest will be perfection—rest from distress, fear, hurt, pain, sickness, and brokenness. It will be a permanent rest from our earthly pursuits that tire us and wear us out. Mostly, it will be like the Garden of Eden, where we once again walk in perfection with our Lord, talking to Him and enjoying His creation with no fear (and no sneaky serpent).

Nothing Wasted

I reflect on my Christian wilderness wanderings, and I wish I hadn't stayed there for so long, but the Lord is faithful to His promises—and He is redeeming that period of my life. Back then, my view was severely limited, and I did not have strategies to fight my spiritual enemy, so I took a few significant knocks. I didn't understand how to activate the authority of Jesus in my life. I didn't know I had anything in Christ except a one-day-I'll-be-in-heaven concept. My fear of messing up my eternal destiny was always close. He was not a now God, and His rod and staff didn't comfort me; they scared me. If you resonate with me, even a hint, don't waste time in regret. You need to pack up and move. Your Jordan crossing awaits.

If a stint in the wilderness helps us learn about the God who delivers and saves, it is time well spent. We may discover we need saving because the rote prayer we prayed at church years ago hasn't manifested in reality or power. The wilderness may help us develop character and discover the attributes of God we need to rely on. It may develop holy warriors, ready to take on the enemy of our souls and bring deliverance to others. Or a wilderness may train and prove us before we take on the giant battles of life.

But remember, the wilderness is not your destination! It is time to move into promise and grow deep roots in that spiritual kingdom, knowing physically you are transient, but spiritually, and forever you are seated in heavenly places with Christ when you make Him your rest. From this vantage point, everything looks different! Those enormous giants will suddenly reduce to manageable form, and you will look down upon the enemy's strategies and storm to victory. The Lord is on your side, fighting your battles for you.

This passage is the culmination of our journey through this book. Please let the words soak into your heart:

> *But God, who is rich in mercy, because of His great love with which He loved us, even when we were dead in trespasses, made us alive together with Christ (by grace you have been saved), and raised us up together, and made us sit together in the heavenly places in Christ Jesus, that in the ages to come He might show the exceeding riches of His grace in His kindness toward us in Christ Jesus. For by grace you have been saved through faith, and that not of yourselves; it is the gift of God, not of works, lest anyone should boast. For we are His workmanship, created in Christ Jesus for good works, which God prepared beforehand that we should walk in them.* (Ephesians 2:4–10)

Finally, determine to be like Abraham, Joseph, Moses, Joshua, and David. Listen to God's word above all other voices, no matter the cost. Sometimes you won't understand what He is telling you, and sometimes you won't like it. But He always has a purpose, and His primary purpose is to keep you safe in Jesus, who is our forever rest.

Be blessed abundantly!

It is time to move into Promise and grow deep roots in that spiritual kingdom.

Notes

Chapter 1: Promise-keeper
1. *Bible Hub*, s.v. "Strong's Hebrew 87. Abram," accessed October 30, 2021. https://biblehub.com/hebrew/87.htm.

Chapter 2: The Charm of Egypt
1. "Ancient Egypt," *Britannica*, accessed October 30, 2021, https://www.britannica.com/place/ancient-Egypt.
2. Joyce Tyldesley, *The Pharaohs*, (London: Quercus Publishing Plc, 2009), 9.
3. Tyldesley, *The Pharaohs*.
4. Tyldesley, *The Pharaohs*, 6.
5. Tyldesley, *The Pharaohs*, 6.
6. Tyldesley, *The Pharaohs*.
7. Tyldesley, *The Pharaohs*, 14, 16.
8. Joshua J. Mark, "Ancient Egyptian Government" *World History Encyclopedia*, October 13, 2016, https://www.ancient.eu/Egyptian_Government/.
9. Joshua J. Mark, "Ancient Egyptian Agriculture" *World History Encyclopedia*, January 10, 2017. https://www.worldhistory.org/article/997/ancient-egyptian-agriculture/.
10. Mark, "Ancient Egyptian Agriculture."
11. Tyldesley, *The Pharaohs*, 17, and Mark, "Ancient Egyptian Agriculture."
12. National Geographic, "Nile River" *Resource Library: Encyclopedic Entry*, April 15, 2022, https://www.nationalgeographic.org/encyclopedia/nile-river/.
13. National Geographic, "Nile River."

Chapter 3: How Did We Get Here?
1. Joshua J Mark, "Ancient Egyptian Government."

Chapter 5: God's Children in Bondage?
1. *Bible Hub*, s.v. "Strong's Greek 4990. Sótér", accessed July 8, 2020. https://biblehub.com/greek/4990.htm.

Chapter 6: Salvation Is at Hand
1. Dr. Nicholas J Schaser, "Blinding the Eye of Egypt," *Israel Bible Weekly*, May 21, 2019, https://weekly.israelbiblecenter.com/blinding-eye-egypt/?via=160275c.
2. Schaser, "Blinding the Eye."
3. Jean-Pierre Isbouts, "We may now know which Egyptian pharaoh challenged Moses," *National Geographic*, December 18, 2018, https://www.nationalgeographic.com/culture/people-in-the-bible/pharaoh-king-punished-god/.

Chapter 7: The Lessons of Passover
1. To clarify, the Jerusalem Council did *not* prescribe physical circumcision for the Gentiles. See Acts 15.

Chapter 8: Red Sea Baptism
1. Andrew Grozli, "Water and Word: Martin Luther on Baptism," *Consensus* 39, no. 2, (November 2018): 7. https://scholars.wlu.ca/consensus/vol39/iss2/2.
2. Grozli, "Water and Word," 5.
3. *Bible Hub*, s.v. "HELPS Word-studies, 1295. Diasózó," accessed July 25, 2020. https://biblehub.com/greek/1295.htm.

Chapter 9: Questioning God's Provision
1. Barnabas Piper and Debbie McDaniel, "'The Lord Will Provide': Why is God called Jehovah Jireh in the Bible?" *Bible Study Tools*, August 31, 2019, https://www.biblestudytools.com/bible-study/topical-studies/jehovah-jireh-the-lord-will-provide.html.

Chapter 10: Testing and Mocking God
1. *Bible Hub*, s.v. "Hebrew 6711. Tsachaq," accessed July 11, 2020. https://biblehub.com/hebrew/6711.htm.
2. *Merriam-Webster*, s.v. "yield," accessed March 4, 2022, https://www.merriam-webster.com/dictionary/yield.

Chapter 11: Bones in the Wilderness
1. *Bible Hub*, s.v. "Hebrew 4784. Marah," accessed October 10, 2020. https://biblehub.com/hebrew/4784.htm.
2. Derek Prince, "The Trademarks of Witchcraft," YouTube, March 6, 2020, teaching, 4:55, https://www.youtube.com/watch?v=Cf7EA8w_vQc.
3. Prince, "Trademarks of Witchcraft," 6:13.

Chapter 16: Crossing Over (finally)!
1. *Behind the Name.* "Jordan: Meaning and History," accessed July 26, 2020. https://www.behindthename.com/name/jordan.

Chapter 20: We are the Mouthpiece of God
1. From Ephesians 6:10–18, Jeremiah 1:9, Isaiah 55:11, Hebrews 9 and Exodus 12, 2 Corinthians 1:21–22, and Proverbs 141:3 (in order of use).

Chapter 21: Taking Ground
1. Matthew George Easton, "Entry for Amorites," *Easton's Bible Dictionary*, https://www.biblestudytools.com/dictionary/amorites/.
2. Easton, "Entry for Amorites."

www.ingramcontent.com/pod-product-compliance
Lightning Source LLC
Chambersburg PA
CBHW050308010526
44107CB00055B/2151